My school Governance handbook

Keeping it simple, a step-by-step guide and checklist for all school governors

Al Kingsley

JOHN CATT

First published 2022

by John Catt Educational Ltd,
15 Riduna Park, Station Road,
Melton, Woodbridge IP12 1QT

Tel: +44 (0) 1394 389850
Fax: +44 (0) 1394 386893
Email: enquiries@johncatt.com
Website: www.johncatt.com

ISBN: 978 1 915 261 45 8

Set and designed by John Catt Educational Limited

My School Governance Handbook

With nearly two decades of school governance experience across infant, primary, secondary, all-through and alternative provision schools and academies, distilled into an easy-to-read format, *My School Governance Handbook* aims to make the complex world of school governance simple and accessible to all.

This handbook will take you step-by-step through the basics of school governance, what the role entails and what you need to know. It explains how schools and multi-academy trusts are structured, the key areas of school life you need to understand, relevant questions to ask and, finally, includes a handy dictionary to help you navigate your way through all those pesky education acronyms.

Including ideas and guidance from other experienced governors across the UK, *My School Governance Handbook* is the perfect companion for any school governor.

To anyone and everyone who gives up their time voluntarily to support our amazing schools in the UK – a huge thank you. You have my shared respect.

Reviews

'This book is an excellent governance handbook written by a highly effective and successful school governor and trustee. It is essential reading for any experienced or would-be governor of schools or trusts allowing them to understand the complexity of the education landscape, and create a blueprint for their own education governance journey. Written in an informative, lucid and engaging style, I highly recommend it to the many volunteers engaged in supporting schools, colleges and trusts.'

Carl Ward, chair, Foundation for Education Development (FED)

'Al Kingsley's *My School Governance Handbook* is an excellent and welcome resource for school governors or trustees – whether starting out or experienced in the role. It's really comprehensive, well written and very approachable.'

Neil Collins, MD, GovernorHub

'*My School Governance Handbook* is a great resource for anyone starting their governance journey and wondering what they need to know first. If you're already a governor, it will help you think about the broader activities going on and how you can improve further.'

Hannah Stolton, CEO, Governors for Schools

'I was really excited to be approached by Al to review a preview copy of *My School Governance Handbook* and it's great, especially because it keeps things simple! Governance can be an extremely complex area, but Al does a fantastic job when it comes to laying things out in an easy-to-read and understandable format.'

Matt McDermott, founder, Multi-Academy Trust Association

'Whether you are just exploring what you may be able to bring to a school or MAT as a governor or trustee, or have already set off on your governance journey, *My School Governance Handbook* will prove to be an invaluable source of information for you. Al has very ably distilled a wealth of information in this accessible guide which should be essential reading for all who wish to ensure that good governance is at the heart of all that we seek to achieve for our children and young people.'

Mark Potter, chair of the board of trustees, Thomas Deacon Education Trust

'What a great read – all resources in one place! This book is fantastic for anyone already supporting schools and trusts or for those interested in school governance. This book will hopefully inspire others and provide the tools and confidence to those interested in getting involved.'

Emily Culpin, governance professional, Hampton Academies Trust

'*My School Governance Handbook* is an essential guide for governors to lead our schools with relevance and innovation. There are many areas where Al's expertise is invaluable, but this book manages to be both forward-thinking and accessible for every governor.'

Caroline Allams, co-founder and chief of product, Natterhub

Contents

'I first met Al in 2020 when he provided support to our failing MAT. From the start he gave me invaluable assistance allowing for a successful transfer to a new MAT. Al has a clear vision of child-focused education, and his depth of knowledge in all things educational was priceless. Al has a comprehensive knowledge of governance at every level and was my go-to person for help. His approach to existing trustees was both friendly and supportive, offering strong guidance tinged with a good sense of humour. On a personal level Al has always been at the end of the telephone for me and long may this continue. I have truly never met a more generous and supportive person either in education or not.'
Paul Rout, former chair of KWEST Multi-Academy Trust

'Al is a shining light of the EdTech world. He is a fantastic advocate of EdTech collaboration between school leaders, education systems and the EdTech industry. Al champions and creates opportunities for teachers, school leaders and EdTech suppliers to work together constructively to share knowledge and best practice.'
Caroline Wright, director general, British Educational Suppliers Association

'I have worked with Al since 2013 when I joined Hampton Academies Trust as governance professional. It is an absolute privilege to work with Al who is beyond dedicated to not only our trust, but also to supporting, challenging and improving the delivery of education across the board. Al's generosity of time, support and knowledge of all aspects of governance is invaluable and we continue to raise the bar in our practice.'
Emily Culpin, governance professional, Hampton Academies Trust

'Al is a great leader and thought-provoker. He has incredible experience and insights, and his heart is at the centre of education. He has supported and guided me on my journey throughout teaching and technology, and his knowledge and experience are invaluable to successful education with technology.'
Paul Tullock, Apple professional learning specialist

'I love how Al encourages and inspires the next generation. My pupils have benefitted so much over the years from his generosity, enthusiasm and opportunities offered.'
Martin Bailey, digital enrichment leader

'Al is a pioneer in transforming school learning but has also been a consistent support for many of us working in the sector - he quietly champions the small fish while having a huge global impact. The nicest man in EdTech.'

Ben Whitaker, director, Edufuturists

'Al is a breath of fresh air - constantly sharing learning, always offering a supportive hand and continually pushing out his positivity!'

Drew Povey, leadership specialist

'Al's work in governance across a variety of settings and demonstration of local leadership in the field continues to be a valuable source of expertise for governing bodies to access.'

George Hayes, strategic lead for governance (Cambridge and Peterborough)

Acknowledgements

Goodness, you sit down to write a book covering all the things you have encountered over the years and then realise writing the acknowledgements is actually the hardest part of all. The list is so long; in fact it's far too long to include everyone I have learned from over the years. I often call myself an 'edu-sponge', and having written and reflected during this book, I reckon I am definitely a 'gov-sponge' too. Truth is, 90% of this book is courtesy of what I have learned from others along the way. I am a big fan of co-production and collaboration, and in many ways being part of a school governing body or trust board really does epitomise that. We all work together, it's a collective of decisions and voice, and we join with the sole purpose of trying to help and make a difference.

It's the acknowledgement section of my book so I can't not thank my parents for giving me the best possible education and start in life to be equipped to follow my passions. Thanks, folks! Nor can I not doff my cap to Mrs K for her amazing last-minute spell-checking and who has always accepted that she's married to quite a few schools as well as me and my daily work, so sorry and thank you in equal measure.

I also have to share a huge thanks, as with my previous book, to the superstar Jackie Vernau (and not forgetting Daisy, Buddy and Alfie) for her support in the editorial process of my books and for ensuring I do sound at least partially literate. Thank you so much once again, Jax!

Alongside so many amazing governors and trustees I have worked with, I have to single out the amazing family we have across our schools at Hampton Academies Trust. I am hugely proud to be the chair of such an amazing board but also want to acknowledge the work that all of our members, trustees and governors do for the benefit of our children and community. We have some seriously great people on our team.

I do need to mention our governance professional (I'll get used to that title eventually) Emily Culpin. She is very much the 'glue in our governance' and has been a huge support over the years, alongside being a real driving force in our efforts to keep raising the bar on our practice. I learn from everyone I work with in governance, but I will shout out a few who I have been a governor with for many years, and who have been top of the list for my learning journey - so big respect and thanks to Sue Hartropp, Tony Gardiner, John Grant, Al Sadler, Paul Rout, Tessa Edwards, Kim Garcia, Matthew Patchett, Phil Smith and so many more I could include. Another thank you to Caroline Behan, director of finance and resources at Hampton Academies Trust for having a read of my finance section and ensuring I didn't miss anything important (I had), and to our trust CEO, Dr Helen Price, who I have now worked with for many years. She's an outstanding leader for our trust and I reckon we make a pretty good team.

There are so many more people I could mention; however, I suspect it wouldn't make for a very interesting read, so suffice to say, I'm a lifelong learner and no matter where I go to try to share a few words of wisdom, I always end up learning as well. Choosing to give up your free time to support the greater good is not for everyone, and in governance that is definitely the case, but in the UK we have hundreds of thousands of amazing people doing just that, often with little recognition or appreciation, so to all of you, sincerely big respect and love.

Foreword

A quarter of a million people in England volunteer to govern state schools and academy trusts, and if you are reading this guide, it is likely that you are one of them. So many thanks for volunteering to take on this important role that makes a difference to the lives of children, young people and the local community. After the last couple of years the country has had with the pandemic, more than ever, schools and their leaders need the support of committed individuals who are also willing to hold them to account on behalf of their pupils.

School governing is not a role to be undertaken lightly. It carries significant responsibility, akin to being a non-executive director of a company or a charity trustee; indeed, some of you volunteering at academy trusts will be directors and trustees.

Governance defines who has the power, who makes the decisions, whose voices are heard and how account is rendered. Governing boards provide the first line of accountability in the school system, an important public service funded by the public purse.

Trustees and governors are the guardians of the trust's or school's values and ethos. While of course bound by the law of the land, governing boards can set their own agendas and measure what they value without waiting to be told what to do by the powers that be. There are matters of compliance which this handbook will help with, but the business of governance should not stray from the mission of improving education for our young people.

Good governance needs to be ethical as well as effective, and the Framework of Ethical Leadership in Education should provide inspiration for getting that right.

Asking good questions is at the heart of good governance – asking school and trust leaders the right questions, at the right time, in the right way. But also asking questions of the rest of the board, allowing yourselves to be curious and to bring your own experiences to bear.

You must establish professional relationships with school leaders, based on mutual respect and trust. Take sound advice before making decisions: sometimes that should be external advice. Understanding the organisation you govern is important. Make sure you do not encroach on the operational role that you employ school and trust leaders to perform. Governance is largely a thinking role, not a doing one.

Governing boards need to ensure their stakeholders - staff, parents and pupils - are listened to. The workloads of teachers and leaders have been rising: even more than usual has been asked of schools during Covid-19. The governing board has a role to play in creating a culture in which your staff perform well, are developed further and wish to stay.

Successive governments have made it their mission to improve the attainment of children from disadvantaged families. Unfortunately, there is still a long way to go with schools now serving more families in poverty. Governing boards must monitor this and seek out the best ways for their school to make a difference.

At the National Governance Association (NGA) we are privileged to support and represent governors and trustees, and the governance professionals who serve their boards. If you have a story to tell or questions to ask after reading this guide, please do get in touch. We aim to make visible the crucial work governing boards do to ensure children and young people get the best possible education. Please join us to do that at www.nga.org.uk.

Emma Knights, chief executive, National Governance Association

An introduction to My School Governance Handbook

I'm an avid writer about all things education, normally with a limit of 1500 words, so this is only my second 'proper' book and, given that the last one was called a diary, I could claim this is my first proper book.

So why a governance handbook? Well, the truth is that with a lot of time, effort and Google on your side, all the information you need is of course out there already, but ignoring the time it takes to gather the advice and resources, you need to feel really confident in your role as a governor. Much like the US Secretary for Defence, Donald Rumsfeld, quoted in 2002...

> 'There are known knowns - there are things we know we know. We also know there are known unknowns - that is to say, we know there are some things we do not know. But there are also unknown unknowns, the ones we don't know we don't know.' (Quoted in Zak, 2021)

So, although we can all Google away to our hearts' content finding the governance resources we need, the biggest challenge, particularly in the early days of school governance, is knowing exactly what it is you need to know. You certainly can't Google the unknown.

With that in mind, I wanted to take the 'keep it simple, stupid' approach and just set out the basics that hopefully give you a solid foundation to be an active and confident governor within your school. This book is by no means a research-level guide, nor is it a definitive summary of every aspect of school governance. It does, however, give you the basic tools to understand what your responsibilities are, the questions you should be asking and a plethora of shortcuts to help you navigate those widely used education acronyms.

We need more school governors, we need the most diverse possible cohort of governors, and we certainly don't need policies or edu-speak creating barriers that discourage fresh ideas and enthusiasm around the table. So, hopefully this guide will help you on your way, or if you are already an experienced governor, it will help validate all the key things you know already.

A bit about me

So, I guess I should tell you a little about me. It seems only polite to at least give you a sense of my background and experience, which has culminated in me taking pen to paper and creating this book. When describing my career, it's easier to split it into two neat and relatively equal halves, with both sides rather agreeably aligned and giving me a fairly unique perspective on the successes, failures and potential of educational technology.

On the one side, I am group CEO of **NetSupport Ltd** (www.NetSupportSoftware. com), an international EdTech software company that specialises in providing co-produced education solutions to help meet the needs of schools, trusts and districts around the world. Within this role (which spans 30 years) I have worked with schools and ministries of education around the world, which has enabled us to develop a diverse range of solutions that support many aspects of school life, including managing the IT, facilitating classroom instruction, keeping children safe online and delivering notifications across the school.

All these solutions have evolved as a result of co-creation with the education space, adapting to a changing landscape and, where appropriate, building a platform-agnostic approach to ensure they all work within a mixed-IT environment.

So that's a high-level summary of the business side of AI – 30 years working with schools, ministries of education and school districts to develop solutions that are fit for purpose and deliver on their promises. It's been a real learning journey and one that has allowed me to understand and delve deeper into the challenges (and opportunities) that technology can provide.

I did mention there were two halves to me. Education is an absolute passion of mine and I grab every opportunity to contribute and add value to support the delivery of education within my community and the wider area. So I also have almost 20 years' experience of school governance. At the time of writing this book, I am chair of a multi-academy trust in the East of England, chair of an alternative provision academy and chair of the regional special educational needs and disabilities (SEND) board. As well as working with amazing and, frankly, inspiring people across those trusts, I am also very fortunate to be able to experience and work across the full spectrum of school settings. My schools include infant, primary, secondary, and all-through provision, as well as those for children with complex needs and who struggle with mainstream education and require a more tailored alternative provision.

With my experience supporting multi-academy trusts and my governance background, I also sit on the regional schools directorate's advisory board (formerly RSC headteacher board) for the East of England, and in that capacity I provide support for their work in developing and raising standards within academies across the region.

From my school governance experience, I'm also chair of our regional governors leadership group, and for several years I've also hosted my own blog (www.schooltrustee.blog) where I try to share bite-size chunks of information, resources and best practice for the benefit of other volunteers working within school governance.

I believe that we are all lifelong learners, and one particular aspect of that which really resonates with me is in supporting the broader pathways for young people as they leave mainstream education. So, alongside my trust roles, I'm also an apprenticeship ambassador for the East of England and chair of our regional employment and skills board.

For the last two years I have been a council member for the **Foundation for Education Development** (www.fed.education) and a strong supporter of their vision for a long-term education strategy for the UK; a fellow of the Royal Society for Arts; and an active member of and writer for the **Forbes Technology Council** (www.forbes.com).

As some of you will also know, I'm an enthusiastic education article writer for a broad range of education titles around the world and an equally enthusiastic podcast contributor. Like many working within the education space, I'm only too happy to take part in discussions and debates concerning the effective use of tech, safeguarding, governance and digital strategy to name but a few, and to learn from my peers and share ideas and advice on best practice. I can promise you, chatting on a podcast or panel is a whole lot easier than attempting to write a book, but if you're reading this, I must be on the right track.

So that's me - a happy fusion of life in the commercial and education worlds. I'm also a firm believer in the big Cs, so expect a fair number of references to context, community, collaboration, communication, content, co-construction and creativity in this book, while I celebrate compassionate, capable and confident educators.

On a personal note, I'm also a dog lover and never underestimate the value of a furry friend for wellbeing (I have two lovely dogs that keep me grounded and motivated every morning).

Purpose

So where do I start? Well, back in 2021 we had seen a real shift in the role of education technology being used in schools. The pandemic was the catalyst but beyond anything else, confidence in using the solutions was the barrier to progress. Not through lack of will, I might add, but through lack of time and support in how to use solutions effectively and, of course, measure their impact. Roll the clock forwards and I think we have a similar challenge that's been growing for a while when it comes to recruiting school governors. There are plenty of people who would love to support their schools and undoubtedly would have skills that could add value, but it's still a bit of a mystery to many as to what governance is all about. We really struggle to attract good people to come and support our schools.

I'd probably go a step further and say the only thing worse than not recruiting great new governors is recruiting governors who then leave soon after, either because the role wasn't what they expected or, worst of all, they didn't feel they had an opportunity to contribute and add value. So with that in mind, I really thought it a good opportunity to take my experiences and try to write a handbook that was easy to read, and gave readers the building blocks to feel more confident in meetings, as well as a broader sense of governance and how critical it is to school management. Every year we see more and more expectations placed on trustees and governors and, not unsurprisingly, greater scrutiny of their effectiveness in our schools.

Clearly you will be the judge of whether I managed to help in some small way. Don't expect this to be a Jane Austen, it's most definitely more Enid Blyton, but you know, it's always best to start with an easy reader. 🙂

THE BASICS

Governance: the basics

What does a school governor do?

For the time being, let's not worry about what type of school you are involved with or looking to join, and let's not worry too much about the name of the role, as in some academies we have governing bodies, and in some we have academy committees or similar derivations, but they all amount to the same thing at the core. Just to add context, we have the role of school governors in England, Wales and Northern Ireland, but in Scotland the governance role is replaced by Parent Councils.

I'm going to start this section on the basis of a governor at a local authority school, simply because it covers all the key elements. When we then cover academies you'll see that the broader governance role is shared across three different hats:

governors, trustees and members. You will find out more under the scheme of delegation section too, but for now, it really doesn't matter about your school's status; to be effective as a governor it's always good to have a broad perspective and understanding.

This section is to provide a setting of the scene, if you will, and a basic overview of the role of a school governor. The intention of the book is not to get overly complex with too much detail; just to ensure you have a good foundation.

So, in as condensed a form as possible, **governors are responsible for overseeing the operation of a school: thinking about its strategy and future plans, making sure policies are in place and followed, reviewing finances, budgeting and recruitment, retention, and oversight of staffing. They enable their school to run as effectively as possible, working alongside senior leaders and supporting teachers to provide excellent education to children.**

Being a school governor is a commitment to support your school, attend governing body meetings, engage with the community and, probably most importantly, to provide support and, where appropriate, challenge. They are often referred to as the schools' 'critical friends'. Governors work *with* the headteacher and senior leadership team to drive the strategic development of the school and raise standards of achievement.

Let's take that and make three bullet points to summarise the core functions of governance:

- Ensuring clarity of vision, ethos and strategic direction.
- Holding senior leaders to account for the educational performance of the school and its students.
- Overseeing the financial performance of the school and making sure its money is well spent.

It's important to understand the separation of the role from the school. We don't have governors because it's a nice thing to do; they exist because they are a legal requirement for all schools to have, and provide an extra layer of oversight to ensure we are doing the very best we can in each of our schools. In truth, the concept is genius from a financial perspective for the government: recruit across England over 300,000 governors, representing education experience and commercial skills, and have them work for free as volunteers to support the education system and ensure our schools are run effectively.

As an aside, in addition to those 300,000+ governors in England there are also approximately 23,000 school governors in Wales and 11,000 in Northern Ireland (Wilkinson & Long, 2019).

> 'Trustees and governors are, in my view, the unsung heroes of the system.'

SIR DAVID CARTER, NATIONAL SCHOOLS COMMISSIONER

A governing body

In the spirt of keeping things simple, a group of governors makes up the governing body. Perhaps there is a catchier term like a 'gaggle of governors', but for now we will stick to the official terminology. We often get called an LGB (local governing body) too.

So, in one sentence, 'the governing body is a group of people responsible for the strategic running of a school'. If we think of the standard local-authority-maintained school setting, the governing body is usually comprised of the headteacher, staff governors, parent governors, community governors and governors appointed by the local authority.

As you have probably realised by now, the governors carry out their duties voluntarily and their role is to hold the headteacher to account for the running of the school and the progress and wellbeing of its pupils and staff. If we could pick a few key headlines that you should be able to check off if you are an existing governor, or work towards if you are a new governor, they might be something like this:

- The governing body sets the strategic direction of, and has a central role in, the leadership of the school.
- It should provide high levels of professional challenge to hold the headteacher to account.
- It should be focused on raising standards and promoting the personal development and wellbeing of all learners.
- It should have a clear understanding of the strategic priorities for the school and ensure an appropriate plan is in place and implemented effectively.
- Where appropriate, it should engage effectively with parents, pupils and staff and be well informed about their views and use this to inform strategic priorities for development planning.
- The governing body should have a good understanding of the quality of provision within its school and how the school's performance compares locally and nationally.
- The governing body is fully and regularly involved in the school's self-evaluation process, keeping the work of the school under review, and acting upon their findings.

School governors in England, Northern Ireland and Wales have very similar roles and responsibilities.

The LGB or, as we will come on to with academies, the board of trustees, operates at a strategic level, with the headteacher and senior leaders responsible for the day-to-day running of the school. As described by the Department for Education, the LGB's role is to 'hold [the headteacher] to account for exercising their professional judgement' over the educational performance of the school and for the internal organisation and management of the school (DfE, 2020).

The LGB, alongside the headteacher and senior leaders, must agree the strategic priorities of the school, including processes of accountability and monitoring. As an example, the board and senior leadership team may develop a school development plan setting out strategic targets and key performance indicators (KPIs).

To effectively hold our schools to account, governing bodies are responsible for asking challenging questions, reviewing their school data against national data and visiting the school. For LA-maintained schools, governors also have responsibility for appointing a new headteacher and other members of staff. They are also responsible for agreeing the school budget and ensuring financial sustainability within the school. Governors must be confident in challenging school leadership over financial matters and carrying out internal audits, usually with external support from the LA.[1]

The team at **Governors for Schools** (www.governorsforschools.org.uk) undertook a great survey in 2018, called 'A quantitative assessment of the work of the governors for schools charity'. While the bulk of the report was to evidence the impact of their services, it also highlighted a key statistic that is handy to be aware of: simply, it's tough to appoint good proactive governors.

> '50 per cent of schools stated it took at least two terms to fill their last governor vacancy, with 29 per cent of schools outside of London saying it took more than a year to fill their last governor vacancy.' (Governors for Schools, 2018)

It's a tough ask to expect people to give up their valuable free time to support their local school, and it's even tougher now, as when appointing governors, we need to also think about our skills across the board, so it has rightly become a much more thorough process. I'll talk more about recruiting governors later.

Committees

One thing you will realise quickly is that a governing body (or trust board) can't cover every topic at their full meetings, and to put it in context, best practice would be the full board meeting five to six times per academic year at least. When I see boards that only meet three times a year, it really does worry me how they hope to cover in sufficient detail all the aspects of school oversight under their responsibility.

So, again as part of our powers of delegation, we create committees that focus on specific aspects of the school – finance, personnel, curriculum and so on – allowing them to focus on that area in their discussions.

---

1. Please note, in an academy, this financial oversight and budget setting would be done by the board of trustees, not the LGB.

To be clear, as a board you only have three choices: no committees, standing committees or working parties. I'll cover these at a high level to clarify.

In the case of maintained (LA) schools, you aren't required to have committees, so the full board could conduct all aspects of governance as a group and you could operate in this way. In truth, this is rarely the chosen option and the only time I have encountered this approach has been for the opening of a new school, where in year one they only have a single year cohort, few staff and limited curriculum to discuss. You could argue it ensures everyone is fully briefed on all aspects, but in a full and active school I don't think you would have sufficient time to discuss all topics in detail.

Standing committees

Standing committees are simply permanent committees that are appointed by the board to undertake specific functions. The terms of reference for the committee will set out its scope and responsibilities. In the case of academies, they must appoint at least an audit and risk committee (see my later section on the risk register).

Within the academy structure, you have your trust board as the main decision-making function, so it will likely create standing committees containing trustees for topics like risk, audit, finance and HR, and then will also create the local governing bodies for each school, so in essence, these local governing bodies are also standing committees. Just to complete the flow, those local governing bodies will also create their own standing committees too.

Why do we structure our governance like this and have lots of subcommittees? Well, there are plenty of good reasons and a few include:

- The workload is spread across the governing board; not all governors are on all committees.
- Everyone is equally involved and has a share of responsibility.
- Clear lines of delegation for each committee.
- Potentially reduced workload for the chair and vice chair.
- Staff with a particular area of responsibility can report to governors in more detail. This improves sharing and relationships between governors and staff.

- In focused committees, governors can ask more specific questions, which allows them to fulfil their monitoring role more robustly.
- Meetings potentially can be more frequent, so decisions can be made more quickly.
- Easier to schedule meetings with a smaller group of governors involved.
- Governors with a specialist knowledge or skill can be utilised on relevant committees.
- Committee chairs can report back to the full governing board. This helps use time more efficiently in full governing board meetings.

All this logic does of course rely on good communication and coordination, which further reinforces the importance and value of the governance professional (clerk).

Sometimes a specific topic or project arises, and we need to form a group to help monitor its progress. Good examples include a school considering joining a multi-academy trust and wanting to evaluate potential partners, or opening a new building at the school. In these cases we don't want a permanent standing committee; we need something just for the duration of the project.

Working parties

Working parties are set up for exactly this purpose. Working parties operate just like a committee with a term of reference and scheduled meetings alongside an agenda and minutes, but only exist for the period of the project or task in hand. They are useful for a few reasons including:

- They can be formed with as few as two governors, removing the need to appoint chairs.
- As they exist for a limited time, they can be set up quickly to meet tight deadlines.
- They are intentionally very limited in scope, allowing governors to review the topic in much more detail.

You'll see how all these layers of governance and committees come together shortly when we talk about multi-academy trust structures. I promise it's not as complicated as it might sound.

So before we go any further on the inner workings of school governance, just to add some context and hopefully be a future reference point for you, I wanted to spend a page or two just explaining the UK schools landscape and all the different types of schools we have. After all, I have no idea what governance role you are considering or already undertaking, and I do want to try to be as inclusive as I can in the guide.

School types

You may be aware, but we have quite a few different school 'types' across the UK, and on face value that can seem quite confusing. I am keen for this handbook to be transferable in terms of governance skills no matter what your setting, so we will focus on the concept of your school being largely generic, and I'll try to signpost if the topic we are discussing is only relevant to one specific type of setting.

England

Maintained schools - also known as community schools, these are a type of school administered by the local authority (LA) and are not influenced or controlled by any organisation, charity, religion, or business. The LA owns the land and building, employs the staff, and oversees admission and overall budget. The community school follows the national curriculum and is inspected by Ofsted. We can include foundation schools in this category too (a foundation school is much like an LA community school but with greater autonomy over the operation of the school and its admissions).

Academies/free schools - these are schools that operate independently of their local authority. They are funded by the government but have more freedom over their curriculum and technically do not have to follow the national curriculum, but in practice almost all do. They administer their own admission process, although many, like mine, still use their LA to manage admissions. It's worth noting a free school just denotes the process that was undertaken to seek approval to build the school; once open, it is just like any other academy.

Unlike maintained schools, academies get their money directly from the government, not from their local authority (although it's a bit more complicated than that and the LA do see it along the way). They too are inspected by Ofsted and rather than their LA. They are accountable to the regional schools directorate (formerly the regional schools commissioner (RSC)).

Multi-academy trusts - nothing too complex here. Multi-academy trusts are simply a group of individual schools (academies) that are all legally part of the same central trust. The majority of English secondary schools are now part of a multi-academy trust and half of all primary schools are too. We will talk about trust structures later.

Faith schools - as the name suggests, these schools are linked to a particular faith and overseen by their regional diocese. Some are maintained schools by status and others are academies that are operated by the diocese. Faith schools have to follow the national curriculum, but they can choose what they teach in terms of religious studies. They often have different admissions criteria and staffing policies to maintained schools, but any child can apply for a place.

Grammar schools - these operate very much like an LA-maintained school with the one key differentiation that they operate a selection process for students at their school. This is done via what is typically called the 'common entrance exam', or '11 plus exam', which is taken by Year 6 students looking to attend a grammar school in Year 7.

Independent schools - independent (private) schools in the UK are privately funded and are not free to attend, often referred to as 'fee-paying schools'. Some of these independent schools are inspected by Ofsted, while others are inspected by the Independent Schools Inspectorate. Admission criteria varies and can be selective or non-selective depending on the school.

Northern Ireland

Controlled schools - think English maintained schools that are managed and funded by the Northern Ireland Education Authority (EA) and through a school's board of governors (BoG).

Catholic maintained schools - Catholic maintained schools are managed by boards of governors nominated by trustees - mainly Roman Catholic - along with parents, teachers, and EA representatives. They answer to the Council for Catholic Maintained Schools (CCMS).

Voluntary grammar schools - secondary schools managed by a board of governors, appointed in line with each school's scheme of management (usually trustees or foundation governors) along with representatives of parents and teachers and, in most cases, members appointed by the NI Department of Education (DE).

Integrated schools - these schools invite Protestant and Catholic students to come together with other traditions, to improve their understanding of one another and their own cultures, religions and values.

Each grant-maintained integrated school is managed by a board of governors consisting of trustees or foundation governors along with parents, teachers and DE representatives.

Independent schools - see previous description. However, they are inspected by the Northern Ireland Education Training Inspectorate (ETI).

Scotland

Local schools - very much in line with the format of a maintained school in England, with the exception that it is the Scottish education authority that maintains them.

Denomination schools - like faith schools and overseen again by the Scottish education authority.

Independent schools - see previous description. However, they are overseen by the Scottish Registrar of Independent Schools.

Wales

This makes my life a bit easier as the Welsh school system is very much a mirror of the English schools' structure and types, with the one omission of not having any academies.

OK, so in truth that was just to add some context to the landscape of schools across the United Kingdom, and to reassure that irrespective of the school type or specific badge you wear, the basics of school governance are the same in every setting. There might be some shift in terminology being used (I have hopefully covered these for you at the back of the book) but otherwise the exact same expectations exist in terms of you providing challenge and scrutiny over what the school is doing, how it could do better and how school leaders can show you the evidence as to why they believe they are doing well.

Multi-academy trust structures

I scratched my head hard on this one for a while as I am keen to keep the handbook simple and accessible, and for some, trying to break down the multi-academy trust (MAT) structure can be a bit overwhelming until your confidence levels are up on all the terminology.

Hopefully you have picked up the main differences that make a MAT, a MAT. Just to recap, rather than being a school that is operated by a local authority, a trust is set up as an independent entity (technically it's a charitable company), which can have any number of academies under its umbrella.

In more formal speak, academies are publicly funded schools, independent of the local authority, and held accountable through a legally binding funding agreement with the Department for Education (DfE). MATs are groups of academies that have come together to form a single entity.

Much as all staff working in LA schools have an employment contract with the LA, all employees of schools within a MAT are employed by the MAT, no matter which of their schools they work in. For the purpose of this book, it's also important to remember that a MAT has a singular governance structure.

Having told you not to worry because governors are pretty similar irrespective of setting, in an academy trust we have the added complexity that they operate with three layers of governance. This is mainly to offset the change from having the LA oversight in a maintained school, to being more independent. So, the three roles are members, trustees and governors. Let's unpick them a bit.

Members

I love the quote offered by the National Governance Association (NGA) (2021) so I am going to use that as a start for a definition: **'The members of an academy trust are the guardians of the governance of the trust.'**

The next thing to explain is that the role of members is not exclusive to academy trusts – most charitable companies have members because of the requirements of the Companies Act 2006. All academy trusts are set up as charitable companies so they too must have members.

As the NGA summarise, members hold the trust board to account for the effective governance of the trust but have a minimal role in the actual running of the trust. It is the trustee board, not the members, who are the organisation's key decision makers. However, there are some critical decisions that sit with the members, especially if the trust is failing.

Members are essential to the integrity of an academy trust governance structure. They are the last line of defence from failures of governance and failure to uphold the charitable purpose of the organisation. Members must therefore remain informed of trust performance and be clear on how to appropriately interact with the trustee board. Members sit at the top of the trust's governance structure, as demonstrated in the chart below.

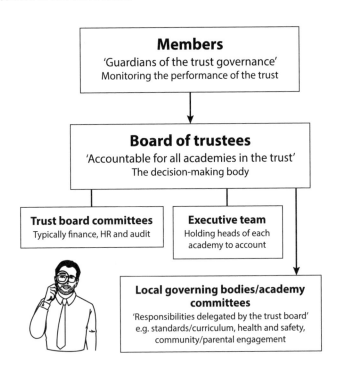

Members
'Guardians of the trust governance'
Monitoring the performance of the trust

Board of trustees
'Accountable for all academies in the trust'
The decision-making body

Trust board committees
Typically finance, HR and audit

Executive team
Holding heads of each academy to account

Local governing bodies/academy committees
'Responsibilities delegated by the trust board'
e.g. standards/curriculum, health and safety, community/parental engagement

In terms of how many members a trust should have, there is a requirement of at least three, but it is strongly recommended that a MAT has five, although it rarely happens. There is no upper limit. Why have five? Well, it helps with having a broader perspective on discussions, helps with being quorate when key decisions are taken (needing 75% agreement by members) and most of all it can help with separation of roles. It's very common to have one or two members who are also trustees. It's a good long-term objective to have complete separation with no overlapping roles, but for growing MATs who need continuity of experience, some key trustees will double up. With that in mind it's always advisable to have a majority of members who are not trustees; after all, you can't really hold your trust board to account effectively if it's all the same people.

As an aside, employees of the MAT cannot be members; that is something that is set out in the Academy Trust Handbook. All member appointments must be formalised, with the details registered with the Education and Skills Funding Agency (ESFA), as well as being recorded in the statutory book of the trust. In addition, the members' names, dates of appointment, and any relevant interests must be published on the trust's website.

For trusts that have a religious character, it is typical that the members will be accountable to the diocesan bishop.

I am probably being a little harsh for the benefit of clarifying the separation, but members don't have that much to do unless the board of trustees is underperforming. Members need to be clear on the limitations of their role and avoid undermining the board. The Academy Trust Handbook states that members need to avoid overstepping their role. The trustee board, not the members, is responsible for the core governance functions and conducting the business of the trust.

Trust board

The trust board, led by the chair, is the decision-making body of the academy trust and is accountable and responsible for all the academies within the academy trust. Academy trustees are the individuals who make up the trust board. In some academy trusts, particularly in relation to academies with a religious character, they may be referred to as directors.

The trust board must operate and make decisions to further the academy trust's charitable objectives, 'to advance for the public benefit education in the United Kingdom'. In trusts that include church academies, academy trustees must also ensure that the religious character of the church academy is preserved and developed as part of ensuring the charitable objects of the trust are met. The academy trustees are responsible for the general control and management of the administration of the academy trust.

As you would expect, as the strategic leader of the academy trust, it is vital that the trust board relates to, and engages, the communities and all its stakeholders. As with all elements of governance arrangements in a school or trust, in the interest of transparency, the trust board must publish on its website up-to-date details of all the governance structures it has in place.

You might remember earlier I showed the three key functions of governance. In the case of a multi-academy trust these fall under the responsibility of the board of trustees, so just as a reminder:

- Ensuring clarity of vision, ethos and strategic direction.
- Holding senior leaders to account for the educational performance of the school and its students.
- Overseeing the financial performance of the school and making sure its money is well spent.

Benefits of joining a MAT

Naturally, leaders in schools will need to assess what they see are the benefits and challenges of becoming an academy or joining a MAT. No two schools are the same, so this is a very subjective process. I should make a declaration of interest: as well as being a MAT chair, I sit on the regional schools directorate advisory board for the East of England (formerly called the RSC headteachers board), so I am active in supporting the growth of strong academies across our region.

Autonomy of choice

Although all schools are encouraged through government policy to become academies, there is not an absolute requirement to do so. That said, the 2022 White

Paper sets an expectation by 2030 that all paths will lead to full academisation. Governing bodies may choose to join a specific MAT. In this case the governing body and senior leadership team (SLT) can evaluate all potential MATs so that they have a secure understanding about their strategy and values, governance arrangements, scheme of delegation and central offer of services and support. Perhaps the most important element here is how good the MAT is in terms of 'fit' for the school's vision and ethos.

More efficient and effective allocation of funds

In the current economic period, schools need to scrutinise best value for money. Some considerations will be to look for savings through economies of scale by joining an established MAT, but they will also look at which services will be provided by the MAT in return for some form of fee (typically a fixed percentage of the school's revenue – often referred to as a 'top slice').

School improvement advice and strategy from school practitioners

Arguably this is the greatest potential advantage of joining a MAT, as it should facilitate genuine professional peer support and guidance, and provide additional support for your school. I'd argue the relationship should be mutually beneficial so you should also look to see how your school's strengths can be shared with others in the trust.

Ability to collaborate and share

Schools in a MAT also contribute to and influence the work of the MAT by encouraging school-to-school support, which allows for additional and broader opportunities for students.

Opportunity to access capital bids

Through a MAT there is the opportunity to bid for capital improvements for all schools via the ESFA.

Review of admission arrangements

There is the opportunity to potentially review admission arrangements and admission numbers. Not as easy as it sounds and it depends on whether you are moving into a MAT that has chosen to handle its own admissions arrangements and operates different priorities in your admissions policy.

Retention and opportunity for staff across the MAT

This is a big one. Certainly now more than ever, talented staff can be given additional opportunities for progression across any of the MAT schools - opportunities that might not have existed in your school. This may help retain their skills and abilities within the trust rather than risk losing them altogether.

Your governance professional/clerk

Be under no illusions how important this person is to the successful governance of your school or trust. In a trust of course, you may well have multiple clerks supporting your activities and they play a huge, if often sadly unappreciated, role in the school.

Your clerk is fundamentally there to support you and your board, to help you to be as effective as you can be. To do that your clerk will likely have a solid understanding of school/trust governance and will help you understand your roles and responsibilities, your legal duties and finally, ensure you remain compliant on all the aforementioned. When Ofsted come to visit, they will want to see the evidence of effective governance across your schools, and it is critical you have someone with a good grip on this.

So, I guess if we try to encapsulate the key function of the clerk within our format of trying to keep things as simple as possible, it would include:

- Keeping the board up to date with changes that you all need to be aware of (typically changes on DfE guidance or new policies).
- Ensuring the key features of effective governance, the board's governance structure and core functions are applied effectively.
- Understanding key national education policies and the local education context in which the board is operating.
- Understand your board's legal duties, such as requirements around data protection, internal procedures, code of conduct, strategic priorities, and so on.
- Reminding the board of its accountability to, and relationship with, other bodies (i.e. the DfE, ESFA and Ofsted).

For academies, they will also know your requirements under your articles of association and funding agreement.

Then come the routine bits: keeping all of us governors organised, scheduling meetings and within that ensuring they occur before specific deadlines for any required decisions. Alongside that aspect, your clerk will help curate each meeting's agenda - ensuring there is sufficient time to discuss each item included, and where needed ensuring everyone stays on topic during the meeting - offer advice on procedures or policy, and in a much broader way, support your chair to be as effective as they can be. I've already mentioned it earlier in the book, but the clerk to my trust that I have been chair of for many years is a superstar and key to our success as a governance team. One of the most important areas she covers for our trust, and something down the line that is key in showcasing evidence of strong governance, is all the 'written stuff' - sorry, that's me getting all technical again. A more helpful summary of the 'written stuff' is:

- Writing up the minutes of each meeting and liaising with the chair to ensure they have a full and accurate record.
- Managing all the administrative processes - dealing with confidentiality, conflicts of interest at different meetings, and the recruitment and training of new governors.
- Crafting the papers for each meeting - not just the agenda, but the minutes of the previous meeting, an action tracker of items brought forward from previous meetings, all the supporting papers to ensure the items on the agenda can be fully reviewed and so on.
- Keeping a record - making sure that if required, perhaps by Ofsted, we have a full and clear chronology of paperwork and records covering all the meetings the board and committees have had.
- Required information - there is a lot, and one aspect is ensuring all up-to-date policies are published for parents to see. In fact, the website has a whole raft of documents that are required to be visible, from your policies to governor details, any pecuniary interests (see definitions at rear of book), as well as evidence of how you spend specific funds provided to your school.

The last bit I will cover has probably already been mentioned above, but is simply their role as 'advice giver' on all aspects of the board's obligations, as well as being the conduit to finding the right person in school when any specific information is needed. When it comes to undertaking any activities as a governor, take my advice and keep your clerk in the loop and everyone's lives will be a lot easier.

In terms of who can be your clerk, the only rules regarding who can't be a clerk are that in maintained schools the clerk can't also be a governor or the headteacher. In academies the clerk can't be an academy trustee, the CEO/executive head of the academy trust or a head at one of the trust's academies.

So hopefully by now you have a fair idea of the role of a governor, a governing body, and their associated structures, you have a taste of the education landscape in the UK, and you know why your governance professional (clerk) is so important. So, what next?

I reckon you are ready to start the next step on your governance journey, be that applying to become one or reflecting on some of the things you should be covering each year as an existing governor or trustee. I won't pretend the next section is an exhaustive list, as in truth there are so many things you could include, but I have tried to focus on the important bits that you don't want to miss.

Your governance journey

Before you apply

Unless you have a child at the school in question, and perhaps even if you do, you may not know the school as well as you think, so there are plenty of things that you can productively do to ensure you are suitably informed before you apply for a governing body vacancy.

I'd recommend you consider a few of these sources of information as a good starting point.

- Read your school's latest Ofsted report to get an idea of how your school is performing and where it needs to improve. You can find the report on the school's website. It's a statutory requirement that it is visible so it's another handy check as to how well-organised and up-to-date the school's website is. I'll cover in a later section a checklist of what information should be published on a school's website, but you'll be amazed how often you find out-of-date reports or policies.
- While you are on the school's website, get a sense of the school's visions and values and how well they signpost their offer. You can also check

out their most recent academic performance, which should also be signposted.

- If they have one, get a copy of the school's prospectus for another sense of their offer.

- Remember, if you are a parent, you become a governor to support the success of the school as a whole. You cannot and must not use your role to influence decisions specifically relating to your own child.

- Take a look at my resources section for some great places to find out more about school governance, but hey, start with this book. 😉

- Have a read of the **DfE's Governance Handbook** – it will help add some extra context around the role (www.gov.uk/government/publications/governance-handbook).

Once you have been appointed

So you have taken the step and are now part of the governing body. It's a big step and I would hope your governance professional (clerk) will have scheduled an induction process so you can meet key stakeholders and have a tour of the school. As part of that induction, you will be given a fair few documents and policies to read. It will probably seem like information overload, but they are all important and will quickly upskill your understanding of the school context and your responsibilities.

Make sure you do the following, just like a game show ... 'in no particular order':

- It's not really priority number one, but you won't learn or contribute at meetings if you aren't there, so get the list of future meeting dates into your diary so you have the best chance of attending all the meetings during the academic year. School evenings are busy, so schools will always plan the dates for the year ahead before the start of term.

- Check out the terms of reference for your governing body. They are written guidelines that clarify the role, purpose and responsibilities given to a committee. These will exist for all your committees, including the main boards, and are typically reviewed every year.

- Read your scheme of delegation if you are part of a multi-academy trust. It will highlight for all levels of leadership and governance who is responsible, and who has decision-making powers for each aspect of school life. Look for the column that relates to you and make a note of what those items are.

- Complete your pecuniary interest/declaration form – this simply lists your business interests and any associations. This provides transparency and ensures you are not invited to attend discussions on anything that may cause you a conflict of interest.

- Get your personal information to hand and get your DBS checks underway. DBS checks are intended to help all employers make safer recruitment decisions. It's a requirement for all staff/volunteers in a school and will check to ensure you don't have any criminal convictions that might make you unsuitable for a role working with children.

- Make sure you have got contact details for your governance professional and the chair of the governing body, just so you can reach out if you are unsure of anything.

- Request a date when it would be convenient for you to come and look around the school and meet the head. And just a gentle reminder: governors should never assume it's OK to visit a school. We always visit by invitation of the head, so you should check in advance.

- Check if the school needs a photo and summary of your career or interests. Some schools like to include these as a bio alongside your name on their websites.

- Ask your governance professional for details of available training courses. Many of these will be provided by your LA but they should be able to provide and get you signed up to appropriate newsletters.

- Get a list of all other governors (and trustees if a MAT) so you know who else is on the team.

- It might take a few days or longer, but check that you have access to your school's systems so that you can get hold of documents for meetings. It's not good practice to email them all out before a meeting and you'll want to be able to see previous ones anyway.

- Find out who the designated safeguarding lead (DSL) and data protection officer (DPO) are in your school. All governors should know who they are. Details about these roles are included in the dictionary at the back of the book.

Join the **National Governance Association (NGA)**. Honestly, you would be daft not to utilise this amazing resource as part of your governance journey. I reference them a few times in the book, and they are a brilliant resource for all things governance, so take five minutes and check them out at www.nga.org.uk.

Most trusts will have their own governance handbook that should set out all the key information you need to get you up and running. As well as an introduction and explanation of the trust layers of governance, it should introduce you to the scheme of delegation and signpost you to the first batch of documents you really need to read. It will be nuanced for each school or trust, but ours sets out these as your first reads:

- Articles of association.
- Master funding agreement.
- Academy Trust Handbook.
- Trust financial policy and procedures.
- Trust scheme of delegation.
- Trust code of conduct.
- Trust strategic plan.
- Local governing body's terms of reference.
- Local governing body's standards committee terms of reference.
- Trust committee terms of reference.
- The role of the trustee and the seven principles of public life.

I did warn you there is lots to read as you start out!

Before your first governing body meeting

Well done - you are making progress and are now getting ready for your first meeting as a governor. You will naturally be a bit nervous about what to expect and whether you will be able to contribute, but don't worry. In the first few meetings you will learn loads, and nobody is expecting you to be an expert overnight.

Things to do in advance of the big night (or afternoon):

- Depending on when you join in the calendar year, your first meeting might be a full governing body meeting or it might be a subcommittee. To make sure you know what the role of the committee is, check out the specific terms of reference for the meeting.
- Have a good read of the agenda so you have a rough idea of what you will be discussing.
- Review the previous minutes. They can give you a real sense of the work of the committee and any topics that are of focus now. If you have time, go back over a few previous minutes and you will start to get a sense of the discussions and themes that are common whenever you meet.
- Check out the action tracker. These are the actions taken from the last meeting, which you will be expecting updates on at this upcoming meeting.
- If there is a report from a member of staff, make sure you read it, and if (as is highly likely) any terms are not familiar to you, look towards the back of this book and it will hopefully give you some plain-English explanations for many of those education acronyms.

At your first meetings

First and foremost, don't get too stressed. If you have already undertaken some of the steps I shared for before your first meeting then you will be in good shape. Key things are making sure you have read the agenda and reviewed any included reports. It often helps to have written down a few questions in advance, or perhaps just highlight on the reports any words or information that don't make sense. You could of course use the section at the back of this book to help you decipher anything technical that has been referred to.

Once the meeting starts, there is a natural (and structured) flow to the meeting. The chair or governance professional (clerk) will run through attendance at the meeting and any apologies for absence (those governors who have already indicated they can't attend the meeting). Hopefully, if this is your first meeting, they will take the opportunity for everyone attending to introduce themselves and their roles to you. Likewise, you will get to say hi and a bit about yourself.

The governance professional will have checked to make sure your meeting is quorate, which is just a way of checking enough governors are present for you to be able to make decisions and vote. Hopefully they will also check and ask if anyone has any declarations of interest, so if any topic involves something you have a potential external interest on, you should say so. Perhaps the school is looking to purchase some new kitchen equipment and you happen to work for a potential supplier.

After that you will follow the agenda, with information presented by members of the school team and hopefully, on the back of that, governors will ask questions or seek clarification on details. Just because you are new, it doesn't mean you can't contribute. Take the view that you are a fresh pair of eyes, so get involved. Also, you might think you will look daft, but always ask for clarification on any terms used you aren't familiar with. We all had to learn them, and staff who have spent time presenting reports want you to get maximum value from them.

This is what some experienced governors shared as their advice if they could go back and give themselves a few tips when they started their governance journeys.

'Be brave; speak up when you have experience of a situation.' Cath Arnold, governor at Rockingham Primary Academy (10 years' governance experience)	'Ask more questions!' Jayne Robertson, chair of St Peter's CofE Primary School (3 years' governance experience)
'You will never have enough time to do everything you want to for supporting your school, so make sure you focus on what you can truly give time to.' Tony Sheppard, governor with 4 years' experience	'Don't be overawed. And your first impressions were right; governors have a lot more to contribute than anyone ever thinks.' Peter Lyster, chair at Honley High School (12 years' governance experience)

Over the first few months

This is hopefully relatively simple, as I think there are two ways you build confidence and knowledge as a school governor (or trustee). The first is by the cumulative experience of attending meetings and reading the minutes and reports supplied. Over time their format and content will become clearer, and you will be better placed to identify changes over the year that are worthy of questioning.

The second and equally important approach is to ensure you get booked onto some governance courses. That might sound like a significant time commitment, but many are a couple of hours in the evening, and in recent years more and more are accessible online. Your governance professional will be able to share details and dates of any courses available through your local authority or accessible through independent providers the school have agreements with. I should remind you that alongside the National Governance Association, The Key for School Governors (schoolgovernors.thekeysupport.com) also offers great resources for new governors as well as plenty for existing governors wanting to brush up on the latest guidance. I am a big fan of The Key for School Governors and recommend it as a resource to any school, governor or trustee.

	'Al Kingsley's *My School Governance Handbook* is an excellent and welcome resource for school governors or trustees - whether starting out or experienced in the role.'
	Chris Kenyon, CEO, The Key Group

As with most aspects of school governance, the official **DfE Governance Handbook** (www.gov.uk/government/publications/governance-handbook) is the bible you should always refer to. If you check out section 4.2 of the Governance Handbook you will see it sets out expectations on your training and development.

Future years

After your first year, you might have a better understanding of the roles of each committee working under your governing body. Don't be afraid to ask to change to a different committee if you feel you can contribute more. It's not unusual in your first year that the chair or clerk will have encouraged you to join a committee, perhaps one that was short on membership, so don't feel that's a lifetime commitment.

This might seem obvious but it's important to reflect on your governance skills as time goes by, and in practice we want to reflect on the combined skills of everyone on our governing body (or trust board), so as part of your future years plan, it's worth checking if you all undertake a skills audit as part of your annual governance cycle. I've included a few checklists in a later section, including an important one for your governance competency, but the skills audit is a much easier checklist typically rated 1-5 based on how confident you feel on each question. The typical questions are listed below to give you an idea and are based around the great guidance from the team at the National Governance Association (2022), who I have already recommended as a go-to source for anything governance-related.

- I have governance experience in a school or similar.
- I am/have been the chair of a board or committee.
- I have experience in developing a strategy.
- I understand clearly what the school's strategic priorities are.
- I am confident I can identify key risks and, if needed, evaluate their potential impact.
- I am aware of how the school is funded and what that funding is spent on.
- I understand budget reports and can ask relevant questions.
- I am clear how the school's curriculum meets the needs of all pupils.
- I understand how the governing board engages with stakeholders and how this informs decisions.
- I am confident being on a panel that conducts the headteacher's appraisal.
- I know how to develop the skills I need to be effective in my role.
- I know what the governing board's core functions are (scheme of delegation).
- I understand how the board delegates its work to committees.
- I feel confident serving on a panel if needed.
- I am aware of the board's legal responsibilities.
- I am confident to speak up if I am concerned about compliance or behaviour.
- I would recognise when independent, expert advice may be required.
- I know, and can identify with, the community we serve.
- I understand the legal responsibilities of governing boards in relation to equalities.

- I have influenced an organisation's culture of equality and diversity.
- I have knowledge, experience or training that will help me to promote diversity and inclusion.
- I can confidently challenge behaviour, attitudes and practices which are detrimental to creating an inclusive culture.

And a few questions to help shape future CPD (continuous professional development) which will hopefully feedback through your governance professional (clerk):

- Is there any training or support you would like to help increase your contribution to promoting equality and diversity in your school?
- What do you need to do over the next 12 months to increase your governance knowledge and skills?
- What specific skills or experience do you have that could be utilised by the board?

I'm an unashamed lifelong learner; I never claim to be an expert on anything, as the more I learn, the more I discover I don't know. I hope being a governor will spark an interest in you on all sorts of different aspects of education, and I cannot encourage you enough to remember to keep looking outside for ideas and advice, not just from within your governing body. I rely heavily on my PLN (personal learning network) and access relevant information and support from other sources, largely through Twitter, LinkedIn and Facebook, governor groups, and by following key education publications like *SecEd* (www.sec-ed.co.uk) and *Schools Week* (www. schoolsweek.co.uk).

For your broader professional development, I mentioned them earlier but make sure you have membership of the **National Governance Association**. They have about as many resources as any school governor could possibly need. I can't recommend the resource highly enough. Alongside the NGA (sorry for mentioning again), I also really recommend **The Key for School Governors**. Many schools have a membership, which allows access to different sections of their resources for both governors and staff. I know I mentioned this a few times, but it's good to provide an extra nudge!

If you are looking at ways to better organise your school governance paperwork, comms, meeting resources and more, then **GovernorHub** (under the same umbrella organisation as The Key for School Governors) is definitely worth checking out (www.governorhub.com). I'm told The Key for School Governors will soon become 'GovernorHub Knowledge' and be part of the same platform/even more closely integrated. GovernorHub also provides a useful governance news website, The Hoot, with lots of useful blogs, articles and information about relevant webinars and podcasts, to help you feel part of the wider governance community. It's a great all-in-one solution that I have used at two different trusts now, and it gets a big thumbs up from me. It's definitely worth sharing those with your governance professional if you don't use them. We also use SharePoint as part of Office 365 at my main trust and that works great too, so it's down to personal preference and really needs the steer from your governance professional.

I'd also recommend checking out the **Multi-Academy Trust Association (MATA)** (www.matassociation.org), which is an excellent resource for trust leaders to network and offers some great events you can attend.

> 'MATA is a new and upcoming association within the space that supports current and aspiring trust leadership, something we continue to recognise is the importance of a great trustee and governing board when it comes to school improvement and trust success. MATA aids this by providing a free membership platform where we provide resources, fortnightly discussion panels and support to the wider trust network! We are proud to support such a great, hardworking sector.' Matt McDermott, founder.

Questions you could be asking

We all know that when someone is new to school governance it can be a daunting time attending the first few meetings, and often the concern is whether you can add value from the start.

The truth, of course, is that anyone can add value, if only by asking the simple question of 'why?' Why do we do that, why are you proposing this change and why have we always done it this way? Hopefully, the answers provided convince you the reasons are sound, but it's a great starting point to understand the workings of the school leadership.

There are plenty more questions that can be useful for a new school governor, and I have compiled a few below as a good starter. The list, of course, is not exhaustive, and there will be plenty of other great ideas that could also be included.

- Have we completed a skills audit that informs the governing body on which skills we want to add to our team, either via governor appointments or by attending training? Are we as effective as we could be?
- How well do we understand our roles and responsibilities based on this scheme of delegation?
- Do we have an experienced clerk who provides policy advice and oversees the governing board's induction and development needs?
- Is the size, composition and committee structure of our governing board conducive to effective working?
- How do we make use of good practice from across the country?
- Does our chair show strong and effective leadership?
- Does the chair carry out an annual review of each governor's contribution to the board/body's performance?
- Does the school/trust have a clear vision and strategic priorities?
- Have we agreed a strategy with priorities for achieving our vision, with key performance indicators against which we can regularly monitor and review the strategy?
- Are we properly engaged with our school community, the wider school sector, and the outside world?
- How well do we listen to, understand, and respond to our pupils, parents, and staff?
- What benefit does the school draw from collaboration with other schools and other sectors, locally and nationally?
- Do we hold the school leaders to account?
- How well do we understand the school's performance data (including in-year progress tracking data) so we can properly hold school leaders to account?
- Do governors regularly visit the school to get to know it and monitor the implementation of the school strategy?
- How well does our policy-review schedule work and how do we ensure compliance?

- Do we know how effective performance management of all staff is within the school?

- Are our financial management systems robust so we can ensure the best value for money?

- How much has the school improved over the last three years, and what has the governing board's contribution been to this?

I wrote an article for *Headteacher Update* (www.headteacher-update.com) summarising at a high level the annual thought process you should consider for your governing body. Hopefully it consolidates many of the more detailed points we have covered in the previous pages. It was written in 2020 but the fundamentals never change. Just make sure you are looking at the most recent DfE policy in each case. I have summarised this article on page 129.

School year groups

You'll quickly get references in conversations to what key stage that data relates to or a specific year group that is being discussed, and it can be confusing to start with. I have included a summary of the terminology used for different year groups and ages of students as they pass through our school system, so just in case you have not had any experience with schools, hopefully the table below will help clarify the structure and names used.

I do also want to make the handbook inclusive for all our home nations, so I have tried to reflect for all countries.

Age of child	England key stage	England & Wales	Northern Ireland	Scotland	Scotland levels
During school year		National curriculum	Northern Ireland curriculum	Curriculum for Excellence	
4-5		Reception	Year 1	Nursery	Early Level
5-6	Key stage 1	Year 1	Year 2	P1	
6-7		Year 2	Year 3	P2	First Level
7-8	Key stage 2	Year 3	Year 4	P3	
8-9		Year 4	Year 5	P4	
9-10		Year 5	Year 6	P5	Second Level
10-11		Year 6	Year 7	P6	
11-12		Year 7	Year 8	P7	
12-13	Key stage 3	Year 8	Year 9	S1	Third/ Fourth Level
13-14		Year 9	Year 10	S2	
14-15	Key stage 4	Year 10	Year 11	S3	
15-16		Year 11	Year 12	S4	Senior phase
A-levels and SCE Highers – non compulsory					
16-17	Key stage 5	Year 12	Year 13	S5	Senior phase
17-18		Year 13	Year 14	S6	

Scheme of delegation: roles and responsibility

Let's start with the quick and easy: the scheme of delegation is your trust's summary of who is responsible for what, and covers all aspects of trust operation.

I would love to simply show you a template and tell you this is what you need to do, but as with most things involving multi-academy trusts (MATs), there is a lot of flexibility on the format and structure of your scheme of delegation. Every MAT is structured differently, so it's important that you look to your own scheme of delegation whenever you have questions about your role and responsibilities if you are a governor, trustee or member. If something isn't clear, ask for clarification from your governance professional or relevant chair.

In a slightly more formal way, I would recommend you look to your scheme when you need to find details about your MAT's committees (including LGBs) and their role and remits, understand which functions are retained at board level and which are delegated, how the trust will support your local governing body, and how (and who) to communicate with in your trust.

I will use our scheme of delegation (or a template based on it anyway) to give you an idea of a format that works well for us. I can't stress enough how important it is that you have seen yours and had a good read.

Top tip - if you are your trust's governance professional, make sure you add detailed descriptions next to individual responsibilities. It will make your scheme of delegation much more accessible for new governors who will be able to quickly identify their responsibilities.

So, step one is defining your governance levels (i.e. boards and committees) a bit like this:

Governance level	Membership	Meetings	Responsibilities	Reporting	References
Members	Five members	AGM + up to six meetings	- Lead vision, aims, strategic direction - Appoint/remove trustees - Approve financial statements - Oversee effective governance	N/A	Articles of association
Board of trustees	Up to 12 trustees including the CEO	Six half-termly meetings	- Ensure quality of educational provision including the standard of teaching and learning - To challenge and monitor performance including student outcomes - To manage finances and property - To exercise reasonable skills and care in carrying out their duties - To ensure compliance with charity and company law - To ensure operation in accordance with the funding agreement - To scrutinise behaviour and safety and levels of attendance and exclusions at the academies - To ensure compliance with statutory requirements including safeguarding and health and safety - To appoint chairs of local governing bodies	Reports to members at AGM and through approved minutes	Standing orders

Governance level	Membership	Meetings	Responsibilities	Reporting	References
Finance committee	Up to six trustees	Six half-termly meetings	- To provide financial oversight and ensure financial probity - To be responsible for setting a balanced budget and compliance with statutory accounting requirements, reporting and returns	Reports to the board of trustees through approved minutes	Terms of reference
Audit committee	Up to six trustees	AGM + one min year meeting	- To provide oversight of internal control	Reports to the board of trustees through approved minutes	Terms of reference
Local governing bodies	Up to X appointed governors including two parent governors and one staff governor	Six half-termly meetings	- To support the realisation of the vision of the trust - To provide a monitoring role in connection with the academy - To monitor standards of teaching and learning - To monitor performance including student outcomes - To monitor behaviour, safety and levels of attendance and exclusions - To ensure that all statutory duties including safeguarding are appropriately undertaken - To act as a critical friend to the head of school - To represent the views of the community	Reports to the board of trustees through approved minutes	Scheme of delegation Terms of reference

... and so on for each committee you have.

Once your scheme of delegation has summarised the governance levels and committee structures, it should also include clarification on key designated roles in your trust, specifically for your CEO, accounting officer, finance officer, external auditor, etc.

Then we get into the main part of the document, setting out who is responsible for what. But let's just pause for a moment and reflect. Because one person is accountable for checking something is done, and one person is responsible for doing it, wouldn't we also want to highlight who else we might want to ask for feedback, or for that matter, who else we should at least tell? Of course, we should, so I reckon it's a much more useful document when we break it down and identify within the scheme of delegation four key actions. In the trust that I chair we use these:

- **Accountable**: the people who are accountable for the correct and thorough completion of the task.
- **Responsible**: the people who do the work to achieve the task. They have responsibility for getting the work done or making a recommendation for approval.
- **Consulted**: the people who provide information for the project and with whom there is two-way communication.
- **Informed**: the people kept informed of progress and with whom there is one-way communication.

I really like these levels, but at another trust where I chair their alternative provision academy, they use a similar approach but with five different descriptors:

- **Own**: the individual/group that has responsibility for determining the task, ensuring that it is completed. Determining the task involves initiating, shaping, and developing it.
- **Deliver**: the individual/group that has responsibility for undertaking the task delegated to them and reporting on its delivery as determined by the owner.
- **Monitor**: the individual/group that has responsibility for ensuring compliance, monitoring effectiveness and reporting on that monitoring while the task is in progress.

- **Review**: the individual/group that has responsibility for reviewing, at the end of the process, whether a particular task has been delivered satisfactorily, and taking any subsequent action as appropriate.

- **Assurance**: the individual/group that reviews the task to test that it has been appropriately completed by the trust/academy. This may be an individual or group external to the trust. Not all tasks require quality assurance external to the trust.

There are plenty of other variations on this theme but hopefully it gives you an idea of how the scheme of delegation is intended to inform all stakeholders not just of their responsibilities, but also all the other aspects undertaken in a school that they might need to be aware of or consulted on.

Then we get down into the nitty gritty of listing all the decisions that need to be taken and identifying who is involved in each of these.

Our format for the scheme of delegation looks something like this (with the exception that ours is also colour-coded by responsibility to make it even easier to scan through).

(Remember: accountable, responsible, consulted, and informed.)

Decision	Member	Trust board	Committee	CEO	Finance dir.	Governing body	Head of school
Appoint finance director	A/R			A/R			
Establish and maintain scheme of delegation		A/R	C	A	R		
Establish and maintain scheme of financial delegation		A	R	A	R	—	
Approve trust financial procedures		A	R	A	R		
Appoint external auditors		A	R	A	R	—	
Audit report		A	R	A	R	—	
Approve budget	C	A	R	A	R		
Sign off annual budget return	C	A	R	A	R	—	

Following my other trust's approach, they use their five accountability measures along the top of their tables with the responsible owner identified in the column, so you end up with the table below for a similar section on finance.

Task	Own	Deliver	Monitor	Review	Assurance
Deliver annual trust budgets	CEO	Trust executive group	Trust board - resources committee	Trust board	Auditor, internal assurance
Set academy annual budget	Trust board	Trust executive board	Trust board - resources committee	Trust board	Auditor
Deliver annual academy budget	Trust executive group	Head of school	Trust executive group	Trust board - resources committee	Auditor, internal assurance
Adhere to scheme of delegation	Trust board	Trust executive group	Trust board - resources committee	Trust board	Auditor
Ensure appropriate insurance arrangements in place	Trust board	Trust executive board	Trust board - resources committee	Trust board	Auditor
Submit monthly management reports (trust)	CEO	Finance dir.	Trust executive group	Trust board - resources committee	Auditor
Submit monthly management reports (academy)	Trust executive group	Finance dir.	Head of school	Trust board - resources committee	Auditor

This works well too, but I think it's easier to find your column, as per the first example, and scan down it to identify everything that needs to be on your radar.

The above are just snapshots of a few items within those trusts' schemes of delegation. It will be a lengthy document, and although it is down to each trust to choose what and how they record it, you can expect to (hopefully) see responsibilities broken down under each of these types of sections.

- Overarching governance
- Strategy and leadership
- Education
- Behaviour, attendance and inclusion
- Finance
- Compliance
- Estates
- Human resources
- Communications
- Safeguarding.

Look at yours, make sure you can see your areas of responsibility or where you should be informed, and if in doubt ask for clarification. You won't be the first or last to need to do so. As an extra reminder, the scheme isn't fixed; we are on iteration nine of ours. When a situation arises that is new and has never been considered before, we will need to reflect on our current scheme and hopefully add an additional line or two to ensure in future responsibility is clearly identified and agreed.

Finance: understanding the basics

Now, I know the temptation is to immediately skip over this section. For many, finances represent the dark arts and it's one of the roles of a governor or trustee that is the most intimidating. I won't deny, having chaired finance committees for many years, it was often a challenge to get enough members to put their hands up to join the committee. I'm going to keep this as high level as I can, so please don't write to me because I missed a small funding stream of a few hundred pounds; I'm really trying to get at the fundamentals.

As a rule, in a standalone LA school, the governing body will likely have a finance committee where expenditure and budgets will be discussed. In a MAT this is likely handled by trustees and has devolved away from the local governing body. Either way, it's important to understand the finance of a school.

Schools get two main streams of money from the government. Their core funding - known as revenue funding - is the money that is spent on running costs, like salaries. They then have capital funding which is for buildings and perhaps IT spend.

All schools are funded on a per-pupil basis. We have a national funding formula (NFF) to make sure that a school's per-pupil funding reflects several factors including the characteristics of their pupils (like how many pupils have fallen behind), how many pupils receive free school meals (FSM), the geographic location of the school (to reflect different salary costs) and much more.

All state-funded schools, whether they are academies or LA schools, get their funding from the government. Independent or private schools operate outside this system and raise their funding through fees.

Just to complicate matters, even though the government decides on a funding rate per child, it is then given to councils to allocate across both their council-run schools and academies. Local authorities then set their own local formulae to hand out their total allocation between all the schools in their area, keeping a bit to cover the cost of their local services. These decisions around allocations are proposed by the local authority then agreed (or not) by a group of stakeholders, in our area referred to as 'schools forum' and involves representations for schools, multi-academy trusts and governors.

This means that while the government's NFF determines how much money each local authority receives, it is the local authorities' own formulae that determine how much each school finally receives. At the time of writing, the average funding per child for a primary school was, depending on geographical location, between £3800 and £4500 for primary-age children, and between £4500 and £5500 for secondary-age children.

I don't want to get too technical talking about sources of school funding, as I suspect you will just be encouraged to flip a few pages, so bear with me and I'll keep it as simple as I can to serve a useful purpose.

With anything financial, if in doubt it's always worth checking the latest version of the **Academy Trust Handbook** – www.gov.uk/guidance/academy-trust-handbook/

So let's start with the money coming in – that's the good bit, albeit it's never enough!

As I have explained, all schools get allocated an amount per pupil on their roll based on the national funding formula. That arrives with your local authority who send it out to their schools with a bit retained to cover some of their costs to provide their schools with certain services. They might agree with local schools to retain some funding to support other interventions needed.

The money coming to the school is referred to as the dedicated schools grant (DSG). If you are an academy, that money comes direct to you under a different name; it's your GAG funding. I have included descriptions at the back of the book which cover these in more detail, but to avoid you flipping pages, here are the main summaries of both.

DSG - dedicated schools grant

The dedicated schools grant (DSG) is a ring-fenced block of money that goes to each local authority for distribution to schools as their basic funding. Funding is based on an amount per child for each school. The amount varies based on several factors, and in calculating the share of the grant for each school, the local authority will retain a slice of the funding towards the costs of your LAs 'children's services' provision. Based on local board agreement, the LA could potentially retain some for additional support towards their 'high-needs' funding.

GAG - general annual grant

Stands for 'general annual grant' (GAG). This is an academy's main bulk of funding each year and represents each of their schools' share of the dedicated schools grant that is paid to each local authority for distribution to schools.

That's your main block of income that comes into your school each year, but you will see other funds too. Some you can spend as you see fit, some come 'ring-fenced' and need to be spent for a particular purpose. So, what might your sources of funding look like? They should look something a bit like this:

Revenue (your basic entitlement)/GAG	Bulk of your income, calculated per pupil with different rates by age band (AWPU - age weighted pupil unit funding).
Additional needs funding (including deprivation funding)	Deprivation funding is generally the largest allocation following the AWPU funding. All homes within a catchment are allocated a deprivation index of A-F (see IDACI). Based on this assessment, extra funds to the school support a cohort from higher deprivation. Funding also includes the cost of providing free school meals to those who are eligible.
	An allocation will also be made for those who have been eligible for free school meals in the last six years (Ever 6 FSM) to help provide additional support. It might also include funds for your EAL (English as an additional language) students too.
School-led funds and extra-premises-led funding	Includes a lump sum per school to support premises costs. Extra funding is provided for specific circumstances, perhaps being on the fringe of London, operating a PFI contract or having a split site for your school, which is more costly to run.
Pupil premium (PP)	Extra funding for children from families that qualify for free school meals (or have done so in the last six years); in essence, low-income households.
PE and sport premium	To support physical activities and workshops - only applies to primary schools.
Universal infant free school meals (UIFSM)	Funding to cover the cost of providing free school meals for all children in Reception through to Year 2 regardless of household income.
High needs funding	Funding received for pupils who have an EHCP (education and health care plan). The amount of funding will be identified on the pupil's plan and will be used to support their individual needs.
Post-16 funding	Post-16 funding is also allocated on a per-pupil basis using a national funding rate and basic formula of additional funding including deprivation.

And that's pretty much it. That's your income sorted, although for completeness you might access other funds during the year for specific projects (to help repair an old roof, for example) and might have some funds coming in from lettings of your school facilities and for children paying for their school meals.

To offset that income, you will have a similar (hopefully not larger) number of outgoings. In truth, for most schools 75-80% of your costs will be staff costs, and as an academy, being above 80% is seen as a red flag to your financial stability. A sudden increase in staff pay could have a significant impact on your budget. If you want to review and compare your costs to other similar schools, then the DfE provide a really useful schools financial benchmarking resource which allows you to pull up your school's data and compare to other schools in your area.

https://schools-financial-benchmarking.service.gov.uk/

(You can compare all aspects of your expenditure against statistically similar schools to see where your costs might vary.)

The main 'people' outgoings you can expect to see on your budget report will be:

Staff costs - teaching	Hopefully the sum of these combined is in the 70-80% range as a percentage of revenue.
Staff costs - curriculum support	
Staff costs - non-curriculum	
Apprenticeship levy	
Agency staff costs	This can have a big impact on your budget and is linked to sustained periods of staff absence (it's teachers to cover your absent teachers).
Cleaning staff	May be directly employed or through an agency.

Then you will have all the typical operational costs making up the remainder of your outgoings.

- Educational supplies/curriculum resources
- Exam fees - this can be a big cost
- Staff development/training courses

- Technology costs – software subscriptions and low value tech
- Travel and subsistence
- Maintenance costs (premises and equipment)
- Cleaning costs/supplies
- Water rates
- Energy costs (I've seen real turbulence here)
- Insurances
- Security costs
- Catering (another one to monitor for changes and viability)
- Bank charges/interest
- Professional services (legal/financial).

You may have a more detailed summary presented to you, but as you will see, on the cost side it's not dissimilar to any business accounts and should be easy to identify where your costs are running ahead of your budget expectations, or where unexpected costs arise.

What should you look for in your school budget?

When you attend a finance meeting, the report you are handed (hopefully well in advance to review) should have an overview of the budget to date – i.e. the 'headline figures' of all the money your school has received and spent at the time of the report. Most, not all, of your budget gets spent pretty consistently through the year, not least because staff costs make up such a big percentage, so if you look at your spend to date it should equal (roughly) how many months of the year you are through. So, if you are looking at a report for the first three months of the financial year, you would expect most consistent costs to be at 1/4 of the budget amount. It's just a simple litmus test to apply.

Don't forget your financial year starts in April for maintained schools and September for academies.

The report should summarise any significant changes since the last meeting and provide some notes to explain things like:

- Whether any anticipated costs have changed since the last meeting and why.
- Whether these changes were planned or expected (and if not, why).
- What the consequences of the changes are to your overall budget and finances.

It will also summarise expenditure to date, how much you have left in the budget and physically in your bank account, and an updated forecast of how you will end the year. The last bit naturally is important.

Have a scan and firstly just look for any significant variations, any high balances where spend is well ahead of forecast for the year and anything that is forecasting an overspend or deficit for the year.

When you are looking at your schools' budgets, especially when a new set are being presented for approval, there are lots of questions you could think about asking. I have added a few below but look for those obvious changes compared to last year and start with them.

QUICK CHECKLIST

- Are our assumptions on staff costs robust enough to handle variations in projected pupil numbers? If we have 20 less children than planned in Reception or Year 7, are we still viable?
- How realistic is the proposed budget? Why are you confident?
- Have we included projected changes in both pupil funding costs and possible staff pay awards? (If so, what percentages have we used for our assumptions?)
- Are we happy we have sufficient funding to deliver the curriculum in terms of staffing and resources?
- What risk (if any) have we considered within the budget?

- Have we reviewed any external contracts recently and how do we know they are still best value? Think cleaning, catering, etc.
- Have we benchmarked any of our costs against similar schools?
- What are our overall staff costs as a percentage of income? (Ideally <80%.)
- What is our teacher contact ratio (percentage of working hours spent teaching)?
- Are we confident in our pupil numbers for September? (See earlier question.)
- What assumptions in the budget are there for FSM/PP children next year?
- What funding will be received next year for SEND?

Hopefully they will help as a few common questions, but as always with anything to do with school finance, if you look for the big variances you won't go too far wrong, and the process of asking questions will likely get full and detailed responses, so indirectly, you will be helping the oversight of your school finance and helping provide evidence of challenge and scrutiny. 99% of the time your finance team will have good reasons for all the numbers and be able to reassure you. What we hope to do is find the 1% where we might have collectively missed something.

Safeguarding: what you need to know

Schools nowadays have so much more responsibility than simply educating our children; their social, emotional and mental health (SEMH) is (rightfully so) a high priority, as is recognising the inevitable balance of opportunities and risks that the digital world presents. Before I go any further here, there is no denying that the most important tools for keeping our children safe are the eyes and ears of both parents and professionals.

I've tried to break this section down into a few key areas that we now know are the building blocks to keeping children safe: our moral and legal obligations; the availability of constantly evolving technology to support those obligations; the practical approaches schools can adopt; the critical task of equipping our children as digital citizens; and online resources relevant to this key subject.

It goes without saying that anyone involved in education supports the view that every child matters and does everything they can to provide a safe environment where every child can thrive. As with everything in education, we have legislation and policies that shape the expectations of our sector. When it comes to digital and online safety, the key ones I will cover here are for the UK – KCSIE (Keeping Children Safe in Education, 2022); Prevent duty (Counterterrorism and Security Act, 2015) – and for the US – CIPA (the Children's Internet Protection Act, 2000).

Keeping children safe in education 2022

Statutory guidance for schools and colleges

Keeping Children Safe in Education (KCSIE) - UK

Usually updated annually (at the time of writing, the latest version of KCSIE was for September 2022), this covers statutory guidance for schools and colleges on safeguarding, safer recruitment, handling allegations, the role of the designated safeguarding lead and (of relevance in the context of my personal experiences) Annex D - online safety. (Online safety guidance is now fully integrated in part two and in Annex C and Annex D.)

Now, I know that everyone working in English schools will have been required to read KCSIE annually, but on the basis that it is possible readers may not be too familiar with or new to governance, I am covering the salient points for completeness:

- You need to know and understand your duties set out in part two of KCSIE.
- Ensure that you have a school-wide approach to safeguarding.
- You need to make sure that all staff who work directly with children read KCSIE and they have confirmed so.
- You check to make sure all staff in your school receive regular safeguarding and child protection training (including online safety) - this is normally done at the start of each academic year.
- Check your school has policies and procedures in place that support safeguarding, including policies on related items such as child protection, pupil behaviour, staff behaviour and safer recruitment.

- Check to make sure you have systems in place for identifying students with mental health problems, including how any issues might be escalated.

- You should make sure students are taught about safeguarding, including online safety, in appropriate ways for their needs and stage. This includes thinking about digital citizenship (DigCit).

- You should check to ensure a suitable senior staff member is appointed as the designated safeguarding lead (DSL).

- Ensure that you as governors and trustees also receive appropriate safeguarding and child protection training as part of your induction and your ongoing role.

You might choose to elect a governor who is a link governor with a specific responsibility for safeguarding. Ideally, they will be fairly experienced and senior in your governing body with a good understanding of your responsibilities as governors or trustees, and at a high level they will be responsible for checking (and feeding back) the following:

- Making sure they keep up to date with statutory guidance and advice from third parties.

- Making sure your school has appropriate and up-to-date policies for child protection, staff behaviour and for handling any allegations against staff.

- Supporting the governing body to improve their understanding of their safeguarding responsibilities and, as already mentioned, reporting back to the board about any safeguarding issues.

- Meeting regularly with the designated safeguarding lead (DSL) to monitor your school's policies and procedures, and check that everyone across the school has had relevant and appropriate training.

- Undertaking a regular annual check (or more frequent if practical) of the single central record with the DSL to make sure your school is undertaking all the appropriate recruitment checks.

I know what you might be thinking: 'Al, you just mentioned a single central record, what's that all about?' Well, I could encourage you to navigate to the rear of this book that includes explanations for many edu terms and acronyms, but in the spirit of minimising page flicks, I'll summarise briefly below.

The single central record (SCR) is a statutory requirement under KCSIE for all schools and academies to keep and maintain a single central record of all their recruitment and vetting checks for all staff (including relevant volunteers, supply teachers, agency and third-party staff, and teacher trainees on salaried routes). It will also contain similar information for the governing body of your school/trustees. It should include your DBS checks too that I mentioned earlier in the book as you got started on your governance journey.

If you are the link governor for safeguarding and this falls under your remit, you might want to consider asking a few of these questions if it's new territory for you.

- Where do we store the single central record (SCR)?
- Is it secure?
- What is the process for maintaining it?
- How often do we check the SCR?
- When was the last time we (governors) checked the SCR?
- Have we or anyone else checked the information recorded on the SCR for errors?
- Are we sure that all new staff are recorded?
- Are there any gaps on the register against any listed person?

I should stress, your Ofsted inspection team **WILL** check this and if they find issues you are not going to have a pleasant 1-2 days with them.

I have included below - broken down into three sections to allow for the format of this book - a simple example of what might be recorded in your schools SCR.

Identity

Mandatory	Mandatory	Mandatory	Mandatory	Optional
Name	Address	DOB	Date address ID seen	Date photo ID seen

Position held

Mandatory	Mandatory
Date started with school	Job title (e.g. teacher/ parent/ helper/ admin)

Qualifications and registration

Mandatory	Mandatory	Mandatory	Mandatory
Teaching qualifications required (Yes/No)	If required, teaching qualifications evidenced	If required, date teaching qualifications seen	If required, date GTC registration seen

Right to work in the UK

Mandatory	Mandatory	Mandatory
Date passport/ visa/work permit evidenced for right to work in the UK	If required, date visa or work permit expires (earliest date)	If required, most recent date work permit or visa evidenced

Vetting checks

Mandatory	Mandatory	Mandatory	Mandatory	Mandatory	Optional	Optional
Date Children's Barred List checked	Date DBS evidenced and checked	If DBS checked, DBS disclosure number	Overseas police check/ Certificate of Good Conduct required (Yes/No only)	If required, DBS overseas checks completed (Yes/No only)	Does disqualification under the Childcare Act 2006 apply to this role? (Yes/No)	If required, date check in relation to the Childcare Act 2006 was completed or any risks and control measures (recorded in personal file) were put in place

References

Optional	Optional
Date satisfactory reference one completed	Date satisfactory reference two completed

Teacher prohibition check

Mandatory	Mandatory	Mandatory
Date of check	Outcome	Evidence checked by

While you are chatting with your DSL in your role as the safeguarding link governor, or frankly whenever there is a discussion around safeguarding, here are some good questions to consider. They are all quite open-ended so your reassurance will come from the breadth of their answers. Consider dipping into a few of these for your conversation:

- Do all our students feel safe and protected and how do we know?
- Are we confident that all our policies are accessible and understood by everyone?
- What systems do we have in place right now that ensure a student can report any concerns or abuse? How do we ensure they are treated seriously?
- What systems do we have in place for identifying any mental health issues? Do all staff understand this?
- How do we ensure all responsible staff in the school are clear on the process and procedure when they are concerned about the safety of a child?
- Tell me about the ongoing training our staff receive.
- What about the handling of any allegations raised against a member of staff?
- What about safer recruitment? What processes do we have in place?
- How is discrimination addressed in our school?
- How do we address child-on-child abuse?
- What system do we have in place to provide online safety/filtering/ monitoring?
- How have we implemented the Prevent duty guidance? Is everyone clear on any procedures we have?

I did mention in the checklist above tools to support online safety, as well as how easy it is for a child to report a concern. We need to be aware first that the use of technology has become a significant component of many safeguarding issues: child sexual exploitation, radicalisation, sexual predation (technology often provides the platform that facilitates harm). An effective approach to online safety empowers a school or college to protect and educate the whole school or college community in their use of technology and establishes mechanisms to identify, intervene in and escalate any incident where appropriate.

The breadth of issues classified within online safety is considerable, but can be categorised into three areas of risk:

- **Content**: being exposed to illegal, inappropriate, or harmful material. For example, pornography, fake news, racist or radical and extremist views.
- **Contact**: being subjected to harmful online interaction with other users. For example, commercial advertising as well as adults posing as children or young adults.
- **Conduct**: personal online behaviour that increases the likelihood of, or causes, harm. For example, making, sending and receiving explicit images, or online bullying.

And on page 36, section 140 of KCSIE:

'Whilst considering their responsibility to safeguard and promote the welfare of children and provide them with a safe environment in which to learn, governing bodies and proprietors should be doing all that they reasonably can to limit children's exposure to the above risks from the school's or college's IT system. As part of this process, governing bodies and proprietors should ensure their school or college has appropriate filters and monitoring systems in place. [Emphasis added.] Governing bodies and proprietors should consider the age range of their children, the number of children, how often they access the IT system and the proportionality of costs vs risks.
'The appropriateness of any filters and monitoring systems are a matter for individual schools and colleges and will be informed, in part, by the risk assessment required by the Prevent Duty.' (DfE, 2022c)

I am slightly biased, but having spent 30 years developing solutions, with schools, for schools, the most flexible and robust solution to deliver the online safety monitoring is **classroom.cloud** (www.classroom.cloud). I helped develop the solution, so full transparency, but I am hugely proud of it and the positive impact it has had around the world in protecting our learners. Please share with your school IT team and say, 'AI says you need to take a look.' 🙂

Prevent duty - UK

Just to close the loop I should also provide a bit more context around the Prevent duty guidance I mentioned earlier. It sits under the Counterterrorism and Security Act 2015. It was released by the UK government in March 2015, and the guidance was made a legal requirement on 1 July 2015. It requires schools (and other specified bodies) to put measures in place to 'prevent people from being drawn into terrorism' (DfE, 2015).

Within the guidance there are four key areas where schools need to demonstrate appropriate action:

- **Staff training**: the designated safeguarding lead needs to undertake Prevent awareness training (WRAP) to be able to provide advice and support for other members of staff.
- **IT policies**: the need for school leaders to ensure that children are safe from terrorist and extremist material when accessing the internet in schools.
- **Working in partnership**: working with local safeguarding children boards (LSCBs) who can provide advice and support to schools on implementing the duty.
- **Risk assessment**: the need to assess the risk of/identify children in danger of being drawn into terrorism.

You can find out more here: revised Prevent duty guidance for England and Wales - (www.gov.uk/government/publications/prevent-duty-guidance/revised-prevent-duty-guidance-for-england-and-wales).

Finally, a slightly more technical bit, but schools should make sure all staff have access to the latest versions of each of these documents. Never hurts to ask as a double check.

- Working Together to Safeguard Children (DfE)
- Keeping Children Safe in Education (DfE)
- Teaching Online Safety in Schools (DfE)
- Mental Health and Behaviour in Schools (DfE)
- The Prevent duty (Home Office)

- Children Missing Education (DfE)
- Designated Teacher for Looked-after and Previously Looked-after Children (DfE)

There was a great summary guide written by Elizabeth Rose – an independent safeguarding consultant and director of **So Safeguarding** (www.sosafeguarding. co.uk) – for *SecEd* magazine entitled 'How can schools establish a culture of safeguarding?' It's definitely worth a read and I'll include the link below and in my references section. In the article she neatly broke down the top 10 areas for you to consider to create your own effective and strategic plan for safeguarding, which I have listed below:

☐ Behaviour and safeguarding
☐ The curriculum
☐ Managing concerns about members of staff
☐ Child-on-child abuse
☐ Governors
☐ Radicalisation and extremism
☐ Pupil voice
☐ Mental health
☐ Attendance and children missing from education
☐ Planning ahead.

You will notice governors are on that list. In her article she explains:

'Governors and trustees have a very important role to play in safeguarding and significant statutory roles, as outlined in Part 2 of KCSIE. It is essential that they are confident in their role, understand what should be happening in schools in relation to safeguarding, and have the skills and knowledge to both support and challenge staff.

'As such, safeguarding training for governors is crucial. The governance handbook (DfE) states that: 'It is best practice if everyone on the board has safeguarding training, to make sure they have the knowledge and information needed to perform their functions, understand their responsibilities and assure themselves that their own organisation's safeguarding arrangements are robust.

'... KCSIE from September 2022 will stipulate that governors and trustees should receive "appropriate" safeguarding and child protection training at induction and that this training should be regularly updated. This will be happening to varying degrees in different schools currently, with some governors attending local authority training, some attending training online and some attending the whole-school annual update training.

'... By considering this now and planning for governors to attend specific training in September, schools will ensure that they are immediately responding to the updated guidance and governors and trustees will be equipped with the skills to provide robust governance in this area.' (Rose, 2022)

You can find Elizabeth's article with *SecEd* magazine here: (www.sec-ed.co.uk/knowledge-bank/top-10-safeguarding-priorities-for-schools-attendance-child-protection-abuse-ofsted-mental-health-education-governors-curriculum-pshe-radicalisation) or visit www.sec-ed.co.uk and search for 'Top 10 safeguarding priorities for schools'.

Digital citizenship

Building on my earlier point around our obligations as a school to put appropriate safeguards in place to keep our children safe online, the most important intervention we can have is to equip our students with the skills to operate safely and responsibly online and in the digital world. For me, that is all about ensuring digital citizenship is built into all aspects of our curriculum.

The **International Society for Technology in Education** (www.iste.org) outlines nine elements of digital citizenship to help students navigate online:

- ☐ **Digital access**: Advocating for equal digital rights and access is where digital citizenship starts.
- ☐ **Digital etiquette**: Rules and policies aren't enough – we need to teach everyone about appropriate conduct online.
- ☐ **Digital commerce**: As students make more purchases online, they must understand how to be effective consumers in a digital economy.
- ☐ **Digital rights and responsibilities**: Students must understand their basic digital rights to privacy and freedom of speech.

- ☐ **Digital literacy**: This involves more than being able to use tools. Digital literacy is about how to find, evaluate and cite digital materials.

- ☐ **Digital law**: It's critical that students understand how to properly use and share each other's digital property.

- ☐ **Digital communication**: With so many communication options available, students need to learn how to choose the right tools according to their audience and message.

- ☐ **Digital health and wellness**: One important aspect of living in a digital world is knowing when to unplug. Students need to make informed decisions about how to prioritise their time and activities online and off.

- ☐ **Digital safety and security**: Digital citizens need to know how to safeguard their information by controlling privacy settings. (Ribble, 2021)

It's not a one-way street either. The benefits of digital citizenship for children extend far beyond the child. When we help children develop healthy practices online, we're also creating a better space for everyone else they might interact with. Alongside that, because technology is so prevalent in schools, the onus often falls on teachers to prevent many of the online risks. Teaching digital citizenship is the most effective way to have a positive impact, reduce inappropriate behaviour and keep our children safe online.

One resource I will give a shout out to is the brilliant **Natterhub** (www.natterhub. com), a whole-school resource for teaching children to be safe and kind digital citizens. No, I'm not on commission, but this is one resource I would encourage you to share with staff in your school. They have a library of 350+ digital citizenship lessons, which are both teacher-led and independent animated lessons, and are a great way to embed online safety throughout your school.

'A great governor is a wonderful addition to a school, and they have the chance to contribute, at scale, to many pupils' lives.

'What's important to recognise is that the generation of pupils in schools today have been born into a thoroughly blended technical era which requires governors to ask the right questions if we are to properly prepare our children, not just to be safe online for that is no longer enough, but to truly thrive in a digital landscape.'

Manjit Sareen, co-founder and CEO, Natterhub

Developing digital leaders within schools is also another positive way to embed the right culture and mindset. Within the context of age ranges, students selected as digital leaders can help to embed the use of technology across the school. They attend regular meetings, support other pupils, sometimes teach members of staff, run assemblies and other whole-school events, and lead on improvements in e-safety provision.

Digital leaders can not only support their peers with the use of technology, but they can also be an active and positive voice on all aspects of e-safety, present reports to the school governors, perhaps evaluate new software or devices, or act as e-ambassadors. I am sure you get the idea that developing digital leaders is an absolute win-win and not enough schools recognise the benefits.

'Digital citizenship has become a large umbrella term which encompasses a variety of definitions. Historically speaking, the digital citizenship conversation begins and sometimes ends around online safety followed by a long list of don'ts.

'Just take a look at the language used in your school's tech policies and you'll immediately know if your school community approaches digital citizenship reactively or proactively. When working with school communities, we start by changing those **don't** statements into **do** statements.

'By changing the narrative this way, our focus shifts towards how to use technology for good by learning how to become a force for good online. Our language around safety needs to extend beyond creating safe spaces online by additional layers to the conversation like digital wellness, and how to prioritize my time online, to how to evaluate the accuracy, perspective and validity of digital media and social posts, to how to be more inclusive and embrace multiple viewpoints and engage with others online with respect and empathy.'

Marialice B.F.X. Curran, Ph.D.
Founder and executive director, Digital Citizenship Institute
www.digcitinstitute.com

Data protection

Unless you have been living in a cage for a few years, I am sure you will have come across the increased regulations and scrutiny of our personal data, and the lovely GDPR guidelines (General Data Protection Regulation). Within your school this is managed by a combination of the policies you have in place, training, and the role of the DPO (data protection officer).

The DPO role involves advising school leadership and staff about their data obligations, monitoring compliance including managing internal data protection activities, training, and conducting internal audits.

The DPO will also need to advise on when data protection impact assessments (see DPIA) are required and be available for data protection enquiries from parents and pupils. Additionally, they need to be able to report directly to the board and be the point of contact for communication with the information commissioner.

The data protection officer needs to be:

- Highly knowledgeable about data protection, GDPR, the school's operations, technology, and security.

- Well placed to promote a data protection culture within a school.

You will have a data protection/privacy policy at your school already, and as a new governor you should check to see who your school's DPO is, as anyone who discovers a breach of data will need to be able to report it directly to them.

I'd also strongly recommend you take a bit of time and check out the DfE's **'Data protection: toolkit for schools'** which can be found here: www.gov.uk/government/publications/data-protection-toolkit-for-schools

Anyway, as a governor or trustee you will want to know that all the above aspects of data protection are working as they should. So as a quick checklist, the things you should be checking (depending on your role) are:

- Privacy notices on websites have been updated.
- Data protection/privacy policy and procedures are up to date and regularly reviewed.
- Training on the above is provided regularly.

Your DPO should have a good understanding of your schools' policies and data protection processes and be aware of the areas where there is risk. When data is lost, sent to the wrong recipient or taken without consent, it is referred to as a 'breach'. You will see below the steps taken when this happens but it's also important to know that when it is something serious or where the school can't remedy it quickly they will be required to report the breach to the ICO (**Information Commissioner's Office** - www.ico.org.uk).

Where your school has a data breach it is typically down to human error and can be things like:

- Sending email with student data attached to the wrong parent.
- Sending progress data and feedback including personal information to the wrong student.
- Staff leaving their PC on, allowing another member of staff or a student to access it.
- Losing a memory stick, laptop, or tablet inside or outside of school.

They are all potentially easy to do, but your school will have a process where any of the above (or similar) breaches are reported to your DPO, who will provide advice on what to do next and ensure the school keeps a full log of data breaches and actions taken. Your log will look something like this:

Data breaches			
Summary of the breach	Reported to ICO	Type of data compromised	Actions taken to mitigate
Email containing sensitive student data sent to wrong parent.	Yes/No	Personal details including home address and health information.	Email training provided again to appropriate staff.
Staff PC left logged in during lunchtime.	Yes/No	Potential access to class list and personal contact information.	All devices set to auto log-out after 10 minutes of inactivity. Training given to staff.

It's important when completing the above that the school makes an honest assessment of what happened, ensures that it is taking data protection seriously and as part of their actions, and has confidence that they will take steps to ensure it doesn't happen again.

You might want to consider asking or checking these simple questions as part of your role.

QUICK CHECKLIST

- Who is our school/trust DPO?
- How do they ensure they are up to date on latest requirements?
- Have we had any breaches?
- If so, could they have been avoided?
- Are our policies being followed correctly by everyone?
- Do we ensure there is regular training provided for staff?
- How do we ensure personal data is not retained for any longer than required?

We also must consider data protection when we are securing new technology in our schools. We certainly don't want to start using a great looking new curriculum app that stores our student's personal information and find out the data is stored somewhere else in the world and open to being shared with unknown third parties. Remember data isn't just text but could also be images and videos of our children, so your school CCTV falls under this umbrella too.

To help us review the suitability of a solution and any potential risk it might pose, we should undertake a DPIA (data protection impact assessment) for each potential solution before we commit to purchasing. It describes a process designed to identify risks arising out of the processing of personal data and to minimise these risks as far and as early as possible. DPIAs are important tools for negating risk, and for demonstrating our compliance with the GDPR. I'm not sure this book is the right place to go into the nuances of a DPIA - it's not that relevant to governors - but to provide a bit of context the main elements within it are simply:

- What personal data does it store?
- Where is it stored?
- Who has access to it?
- How long is it retained?

It's more complex than that, but if you know the above you can then start to assess a risk if the data is compromised in some way.

One thing I do want to add here, no matter whether you are a parent at the school or not, we all have a responsibility for the appropriate use of and security of children and staff data. We don't want our schools processing data they don't need, to have risks where it might be shared externally or to make rash decisions on insecure software. It's good you ask and challenge around this area on a regular basis.

Privacy

We have covered many of the themes that link into privacy above, but I can't stress enough the responsibilities that sit on any organisation that is responsible for processing the personal data of their staff and students. We are all far too quick to share information without thinking of the repercussions that may follow. In schools we need to be most mindful, not just of the security of our systems (and who has access to them), but also what curriculum and school apps we choose to use and how transparent and secure they are with our precious data.

Any potential vendor should have a clear and plain-English 'data processing policy' visible on their website for review. We need to ensure our staff are checking this and not just going through the motions. I am reassured in my trust that our IT manager is super thorough and stringent in his checks before anything gets approved.

This is right on the periphery of what is really needed from a governance perspective on data privacy, but I do believe context is everything, so I also wanted to include an article I wrote on why I believe it's time for a different mindset on digital security and privacy in education. This focuses much more on educating our children to be able to limit the risk to them, alongside what we might do formally with their data within the school.

It's time for a different mindset on digital security and privacy in edtech.

Our children's immersion in education technology isn't going to slow down, which means technology-related privacy and security can't either. We're never going to reach a point where we put our pencils down and say, 'We're all safe and secure now, so we don't need to worry anymore.'

In the very near term of privacy and security regarding education technology, however, where we currently invest our time and energy may not be with the places and issues that will truly help. It's time for a different mindset and by that, I'm suggesting that education technology entrepreneurs, developers and investors step up their focus on privacy and security, rather than place the burden on educators. Let me explain.

Right now, most education technology products and resources zero in on the balance between building an easy, open, accessible and collaborative tool with the other end of the spectrum, building an impenetrable fortress. I'm not suggesting that we reduce our emphasis on privacy and security, rather that we recognize that when the bell rings and students move off our platforms, they are on their own. Despite our best efforts to teach digital citizenship, or how powerful or revolutionary our technology is, when a student leaves the classroom, learning platform or school device, there is very little safety net protecting them.

Students spend a significant amount of time outside of formal learning ecosystems engaging with outside content and with each other, creating and sharing data. Furthermore, they interact with people and data outside of learning platforms far more often than they do within our learning platforms. We know all too well that these socially minded platforms and systems are not nearly as secure as those created for school use.

There's nothing we can do about that. We can't be responsible for the time students spend outside of our reach, however, that answer is not good enough. If we care about educating and protecting students – as all of us educators and education technologists do – it's not good enough to make sure our heat is working and yet send students out into the cold without a coat.

I'm of the view that educating about digital security is just as vital as digital security itself. As an industry, we need to educate just as much as we develop. In other words, we need systems and experiences that teach while teaching.

Here is an example. It may be better for educational technology architects to not just delete the online footprints of students when they exit a remote learning platform, but instead tell students what is happening and why, right at that moment.

Imagine, for example, a pop-up informing students every time an edtech product deletes their data, anonymizes their profile, or verifies a security setting. Not only would we feel better about our products when seeing this in real time, but students may also notice that their video games and chat platforms don't issue the same alerts – one simple step with significant potential to educate and improve accountability. Students will quickly begin to recognize the difference between the secure services their schools use and those that might expose their data, and consequently, better understand the significance of overt and stated actions to protect their data.

Going further, wherever possible, online security and privacy examples can be integrated into the curriculum. It is possible, for example, to teach English or math concepts using best practices of digital diligence and citizenship – teaching self-awareness and a critical eye.

For our part as technology providers, we play a significant role in educating students about the responsible use of technology. Doing so organically, at the moment of engagement is powerful grounding for essential digital citizenship education.

In Finland, which has one of the most well-respected educational systems in the world, teaching online and social media citizenship starts in kindergarten and it is infused in the curriculum all the way through secondary school. Technology safety and security are a top priority and they actively teach about it, equipping their students with specific skills in protecting their personal data.

Teaching digital citizenship will be more successful if we approach this from both sides: the teachable moment when engaged with technology and the overt teaching of technology safety and privacy. For the edtech industry, product effectiveness should not only be defined by how well we protect, but also by how well we facilitate in students learning how to protect themselves.

Originally published in *edCircuit* magazine, June 2022

www.edcircuit.com/its-time-for-a-different-mindset-on-digital-security-and-privacy-in-edtech/

Curriculum: the low down

Ofsted has put the curriculum in the spotlight. Under its current framework, introduced in 2019, the 'quality of education' judgement has replaced the old 'teaching, learning and assessment' and 'pupil outcomes' judgements.

Inspectors now look at a school's broader curriculum offering as a measure of school quality, reducing the reliance on exam results.

In practice, this means your school needs to be clear on the answers to three key questions:

- What are you trying to achieve through your curriculum? **(Intent)**
- How is your curriculum being delivered? **(Implementation)**
- What difference is your curriculum making? **(Impact)**

Her Majesty's Chief Inspector Amanda Spielman summarised the curriculum as 'the yardstick for what school leaders want their pupils to know and to be able to do by the time they leave school. ... The national curriculum provides us with an important benchmark, but beyond it the content and structure of knowledge and how this is delivered is something for to school leaders to decide on' (Spielman, 2018).

Most likely you will have a committee focused on monitoring the curriculum or standards, and under its terms of reference your main objectives will be to scrutinise and report on subject or curriculum delivery, the impact of interventions underway, how well you are utilising resources, and ultimately measures of attainment and progress of your students.

Given one of the main things we aim to deliver in all our schools is a 'broad and balanced curriculum', here are some simple 'high-level' questions that you can ask, irrespective of your experience on the governing body.

- ☐ How is our curriculum shaped and adapted to meet the needs of all our children and how do you know?
- ☐ Is our curriculum appropriate for all our children, including those with special educational needs and disabilities (SEND)? Again, how do you know? What evidence do we have?
- ☐ Is our curriculum broad enough that we provide opportunities for our higher-ability children?
- ☐ Do we work with other schools in our MAT or within the local area to share best practice? If we do, how has that benefitted us, and can you share some examples? (A handy one to discuss inter-MAT benefits.)
- ☐ What kinds of concerns have been raised about our current curriculum and how do you address these from parents? (Likely to be around topics such as GCSE option groups or A-level choices available.)

If you want to better understand the data being shared with you at your governing body meetings (and I'm keen not to make this handbook too technical), then I would recommend you take a look at '**Understanding your data: a guide for school governors and academy trustees**' from the ESFA (www.gov.uk/government/publications/understanding-your-data-a-guide-for-school-governors-and-academy-trustees/understanding-your-data-a-guide-for-school-governors-and-academy-trustees), which is a really detailed summary. I will condense a few of the salient points to get you started.

It seems appropriate here to use some clear expectations when looking at the quality of education, so where better than from the DfE's Education Inspection Framework. These are shaped around those three pillars referenced earlier of intent, implementation, and impact. This is what an Ofsted inspector will be making a judgement about, so as a governor it's a great start to see if you see evidence around these strands.

Intent

☐ leaders take on or construct a curriculum that is ambitious and designed to give all learners, particularly the most disadvantaged and those with special educational needs and/or disabilities (SEND) or high needs, the knowledge and cultural capital they need to succeed in life

☐ the provider's curriculum is coherently planned and sequenced towards cumulatively sufficient knowledge and skills for future learning and employment

☐ the provider has the same academic, technical, or vocational ambitions for almost all learners. Where this is not practical – for example, for some learners with high levels of SEND – its curriculum is designed to be ambitious and to meet their needs

☐ learners study the full curriculum. Providers ensure this by teaching a full range of subjects for as long as possible, 'specialising' only when necessary

Implementation

☐ teachers have good knowledge of the subject(s) and courses they teach. Leaders provide effective support, including for those teaching outside their main areas of expertise

☐ teachers present subject matter clearly, promoting appropriate discussion about the subject matter they are teaching. They check learners' understanding systematically, identify misconceptions accurately and provide clear, direct feedback. In doing so, they respond and adapt their teaching as necessary, without unnecessarily elaborate or differentiated approaches

☐ over the course of study, teaching is designed to help learners to remember in the long term the content they have been taught and to integrate new knowledge into larger concepts

☐ teachers and leaders use assessment well, for example to help learners embed and use knowledge fluently or to check understanding and inform teaching. Leaders understand the limitations of assessment and do not use it in a way that creates unnecessary burdens for staff or learners

☐ teachers create an environment that allows the learner to focus on learning. The resources and materials that teachers select - in a way that does not create unnecessary workload for staff - reflect the provider's ambitious intentions for the course of study and clearly support the intent of a coherently planned curriculum, sequenced towards cumulatively sufficient knowledge and skills for future learning and employment

☐ a rigorous approach to the teaching of reading develops learners' confidence and enjoyment in reading. At the early stages of learning to read, reading materials are closely matched to learners' phonics knowledge

Impact

☐ learners develop detailed knowledge and skills across the curriculum and, as a result, achieve well. Where relevant, this is reflected in results from national tests and examinations that meet government expectations, or in the qualifications obtained

☐ learners are ready for the next stage of education, employment, or training. Where relevant, they gain qualifications that allow them to go on to destinations that meet their interests, aspirations, and the intention of their course of study. They read widely and often, with fluency and comprehension. (DfE, 2022a)

'Good governance is about the people ensuring the process, to secure the performance. Having the right people, grounded in children's outcomes, around the table is an essential feature.'

George Hayes, strategic lead for governance (Cambridgeshire and Peterborough)

To supplement your journey into the curriculum you will (hopefully) find any of the terms discussed at your meetings covered in the last section of this book, where I have tried to provide some plain-English explanations for all the acronyms. Given how many there are that relate to the curriculum, it wouldn't be a good use of paper to include them all here as well, so apologies in advance for the page flicking. I have, however, included just a few of the really important ones here just to help you out.

Attainment 8

Attainment 8 is a measure of academic performance in a secondary school. It is calculated by adding together a student's highest scores across eight government-approved school subjects. These numbers are not made publicly available on a pupil-by-pupil basis. Scores taken from across a school year group are averaged to produce a school's overall score.

The eight subjects are divided into three categories, often referred to as 'buckets':

Bucket 1

This contains English and maths, which are worth double marks, but the English will only count for double marks if both English literature and English language are taken. (Only the higher grade of the two is used.)

Bucket 2

The top three scores from the English Baccalaureate (see EBacc) subjects taken, i.e. sciences, computer science, history, geography, and languages (see MFL).

Bucket 3

Contains the top three scores from any remaining EBacc subjects or other approved qualifications i.e. other GCSEs or Level 2 certificates in some technical subjects.

The grades are then converted into points, put through a magic formula that is beyond me, and finally out comes the school's Attainment 8 score.

Progress 8

Progress 8 is a type of 'value-added' measure that indicates how much students at a secondary school have improved over a five-year period when compared to a government-calculated expected level of improvement. So in essence, how well have they done, based on what we statistically expected them to achieve.

It takes a pupil's performance in relation to their peers at primary school level, compares it with their performance at GCSEs (see Attainment 8 score) and then, after some fancy calculations, establishes whether the student has progressed at, above or below the expected level.

The scores for individual children are not published but they are grouped together to get an average for your school's overall P8 score.

A score of zero means that, on average, students in your school performed as well at GCSEs as other students across the country who achieved similar results originally at the end of key stage 2.

A score above zero means that, on average, students at your school made more academic progress than those students across the country who achieved similar results at the end of key stage 2.

A score below zero means that, on average, students at your school made less progress than students across the country who achieved similar results at the end of key stage 2.

Just to be clear, if your school has a negative Progress 8 score, it doesn't mean there was no progress, but rather that your students made less progress than their peers across the country. Also, this score is dependent on an accurate starting score at the end of Year 6 and does not include the full breadth of subjects across the curriculum.

SATs - Standard Assessment Tests

If you are a primary governor, you will likely have come across these as your main checkpoints in a child's academic performance. The Standard Assessment Tests (SATS) are used to evaluate each child's educational progress at the end of Years 2 and 6. They make comparisons between your children and the average attainment expectations for their respective age group nationally.

Key stage 1 SATs take place at the end of the infants stage in Year 2. The assessments are carried out internally by the teacher and they evaluate ability in reading, SPaG (spelling, punctuation and grammar) and maths.

Key stage 2 SATs are a more formal process than key stage 1 and take place near the end of Year 6. The tests also cover reading, SPaG and maths. The papers are marked externally not internally like the KS1 SATs.

Pupil premium (PP)

We can start with the easy definition: pupil premium (PP) is funding to improve education outcomes for disadvantaged pupils in schools in England.

In terms of eligibility, it is paid to schools for students who are eligible for free school meals or have been eligible in the past six years (see Ever 6 FSM) and paid at a higher rate for students who have been adopted from care or have left care. It is paid to the local authority for any children who are in care with them.

The important bit for governors is (and actually there are a few bits so bear with me), firstly, the funds are paid to the school. They are not personal budgets so don't have to be spent student by student, but it is expected that it will be used specifically for support and interventions for your pupil premium qualifying cohort. The three key areas that are recommended for focus are:

- High-quality teaching, such as staff professional development.
- Targeted academic support, such as tutoring.

- Wider strategies to address non-academic barriers to success in schools, such as attendance, behaviour, and social and emotional support.

But that is by no means exhaustive, and schools will use PP funds to cover the costs of trips for some students, clothing, and all sorts of other initiatives to ensure they are supported. As a governor, however, you want to be satisfied there are bespoke interventions being funded by your PP and that existing staff costs and resources are not just being assigned to the pupil premium pot.

I did say there was more than one bit! In return for these funds, schools must show how they're using their pupil premium funding by publishing a statement on their website about how it is used (in detail) and the impact it has on the attainment of disadvantaged pupils. They will also be measured through inspections by Ofsted and through published performance tables. I would encourage you as a governor to go to your school website, find the school's pupil premium report, check it is up to date and ensure that it identifies where the funds have been spent, how impact was measured and what evidence the school has to support this. It's also a handy check to ensure your school website is up to date and that your pupil premium report, amongst others, is easy to find. I always used the 'night before' Ofsted inspector checking out your school website, seeing out-of-date statements and reports still live. It doesn't set a good impression.

If you do have the pleasure of an Ofsted visit, then as a governor they will likely ask you what your pupil premium funding is for this year and how you know it is being well spent. You have been warned.

Check out this link for more information: www.gov.uk/government/publications/pupil-premium/pupil-premium

Recruiting new governors

Recruiting governors is never an easy task, but it is a process that can really be improved if you know what to share and, increasingly, who to ask. Naturally, depending on the specific governor role you need to fill, you may be looking to your current parent cohort or staff cohort and undertaking an election process, but for most of your governors (or trustees/members) you will be looking to recruit people who bring a good mix of skills that are complementary to your existing governing body.

So, before we go any further, a first check is to ask 'do you undertake governance skills audit every year?' If not, this might be a helpful nudge to do one. I explained the basics earlier in the book as part of your things to do after your first year as a governor. That helps reveal across the governing body where we might have gaps alongside professional experience (i.e. finance, HR, education, project management, etc. will feed into our governance recruitment process).

What's the key to a good governor recruitment pack? Well, as a start you should include:

QUICK CHECKLIST

☐ A welcome letter.

☐ Your school's prospectus for context and any current information that may be helpful (a recent Ofsted judgement, planned expansion, etc.).

☐ A description of the role (including your time commitment expectations).

☐ Some constructive benefits of being a school governor.

☐ How to apply/contact details.

☐ And an all-important application form.

In your letter you'll want to highlight that joining your school as a governor will allow the individual to use their own experiences of education and life beyond school to inform conversations, develop and utilise their skills in a board-level environment, make a valuable contribution to education and their community, support and challenge the school so that it continues to improve for your children, and that you want them to bring their unique experiences, perspectives and insights to support your decision-making processes.

Sounds all rather easy, doesn't it? Sadly, the above is relatively easy to pull together, but getting the word out to as broad an audience as possible is tough. You might want to consider companies in the area that may have staff interested in developing their skills and getting involved, social media groups, and so on.

I have somewhat successfully (won't claim they were perfect) used video clips to attract interest and applications on social media. They always say a picture is worth a thousand words, so a nice snappy video clip to attract interest can work well too. Apologies, I went for the superhero cape approach.

When we shift focus to recruiting trustees, the skills aspect becomes even more important to ensure they complement your current trust board.

The recruitment process is one you need to get right, so increasingly MATs are looking to external specialists to help with the recruitment process and match the right people with your trust. There are quite a few organisations available to support MATs in this process. **Governors for Schools** (www.governorsforschools. org.uk) is a great example with really positive reviews from schools and is very focused on finding the right match of volunteers that meet your needs. They also support and work with academy trusts in trustee recruitment.

GOVERNORS
FOR SCHOOLS

'The aim of our charity is to find and match skilled volunteers with the many governance vacancies across England and Wales. We look for people who can bring a diversity of background and therefore thought to the role, ensuring that different perspectives and experience can enhance conversations around the board table. We believe it is through such conversations that positive change can occur at school and trust level, helping to shape the education system to meet the needs of all pupils.'
Hannah Stolton, CEO, Governors for Schools

They also facilitate annual conferences to bring lots of great CPD from expert panellists that you can access online as well as a range of eLearning modules on many of the key topics within governance.

The Academy Ambassadors Programme (AAP) under the New Schools Network was another useful service. However, that service was withdrawn in 2022, and some of their teams are now at Governors for Schools.

One thing that is key to a successful process once you have found the right person to join your team is the induction process you structure, so they can hit the ground running as quickly as possible. Our trust undertook a review recently to ensure we had a good structure and checklist for any new trustees or governors. I have shared a copy below which may be helpful, but credit to Emily Culpin, our trust governance professional at Hampton Academies Trust (www.hamptonacademiestrust.org.uk) for this.

Trustee/governor induction

'The members, board of trustees, chief executive officer (CEO), local governing body and head of school believe it is essential that all new trustees and local governors receive a comprehensive induction package covering a broad range of issues and topics. There is a commitment to ensure that new trustees and governors are given the necessary information and support to fulfil their role with confidence. The process is seen as an investment, leading to more effective governance and retention of governors.'

New trustees/governors as soon as is practicable will:

- Undertake an induction with the chair of trust and trust governance lead.
- Be welcomed to the LGB by the chair and clerk/be welcomed to the board of trustees by chair and clerk to trustees.
- Be invited by the clerk to visit the different school or trust sites.
- Have the opportunity to tour each academy and meet staff and students (where appropriate).
- Be asked to complete a DBS check, governor information form, register of interest form, KCSIE form, skills audit and other documentation as required.
- Have the opportunity to meet informally with an existing governor who will offer support and guidance (if required).
- Be accompanied to their first meeting (if required).
- Be provided with our local authority's governance handbook and training programme.
- Complete the safeguarding and safer recruitment training.
- Attend other training as identified by the skills audit/matrix.

New trustees/governors will receive:

- The DfE Governance Handbook.
- The academy's induction pack for governors.
- The academy's governor code of conduct.
- The DfE's Keeping Children Safe in Education.
- The DfE's Competency Framework for Governance.
- The ESFA's Academy Trust Handbook.
- The trust's safeguarding policies.
- The DfE's Prevent guidance.
- The academy's latest Ofsted report.
- The academy's latest development plan.
- The academy's self-evaluation documents.
- The academy's latest Ofsted Data Dashboard snapshot.
- An outline of any training governors are required to attend.

- Minutes of the last meeting and the details of any committees including schemes of delegation/terms of reference.
- The latest exec head/head of school report (SharePoint).
- Dates for future governors' meetings.
- Details of how to contact the other members, trustees and governors.
- Policy documents relevant to membership.
- The governor visits policy.
- List of governor link roles.
- List of governor committees.
- Governor action plan.
- The academy prospectus.
- A list of common acronyms (or give them this book 🙂).
- Details of how to contact the academy, including the email address and website.
- A calendar of academy events.
- Log in details to the school IT system.
- Recent academy newsletters.

Areas that will be discussed:

- Background to the trust.
- Current issues facing the trust and individual schools.
- Visiting the schools.
- The relationship between the head of school and LGB.
- An overview of the role and expectations including confidentiality.
- How the meetings are conducted, including the use of the governor portal.
- Child protection arrangements at the trust and the governor's role in safeguarding these.
- How to propose agenda items.
- Importance of giving apologies if unable to attend meetings.
- Governor training.

Websites: what should they contain?

There is way more than you realise that needs to be published on your school's website, and I reckon as one step removed governors, we can play a useful function in ensuring we are fresh, current, and compliant. Sometimes the information is there but it's poorly signposted. I try to put myself in the eyes of an Ofsted inspector the night before they come to visit one of our schools. What perceptions might they get about us from vising our website? Do we look organised and professional? Are we hiding important information away? It's a good idea to plan some time to take a look.

This is something your governance professional (clerk) will be managing, but the more pairs of eyes, the better.

So, what do you want to ensure is included on your school's website? Here is a fairly extensive list of things to check for.

Contact details:

- ☐ School name
- ☐ Postal address
- ☐ Telephone number
- ☐ Name of person who deals with queries from parents
- ☐ Name of your school's special educational needs coordinator (SENCO).

School policies:

- ☐ Behaviour policy
- ☐ Statement of values and ethos
- ☐ Charging and remissions policy
- ☐ School complaints procedure
- ☐ Your school's most recent Ofsted report
- ☐ Equality objectives/equality duty
- ☐ Link to your school's performance tables page (www.gov.uk/school-performance-tables)
- ☐ Provider access policy statement (secondary)
- ☐ Time off taken by staff who are union officials
- ☐ Number of staff earning over £100k, in £10k bandings
- ☐ Link to your school's 'schools financial benchmarking' page (schools-financial-benchmarking.service.gov.uk)
- ☐ Your relationships and sex education (RSE) policy
- ☐ Your admissions arrangements for SEND students.

Curriculum:

- ☐ For each academic year, the content of the curriculum for each subject
- ☐ Details of how to find out more about your curriculum
- ☐ Details of your school's remote learning provision
- ☐ Primary: the names of any phonics or reading schemes you're using
- ☐ Secondary: a list of courses available to pupils, e.g. GCSEs.

Admissions:

- ☐ If applicable, statement advising to contact the LA to find out about your admission arrangements
- ☐ If applicable, your school's admission arrangements, how to apply, how you select students, oversubscription criteria, appeal process and in-year admissions.

Pupil premium (PP) summary:

- ☐ Details of how it was spent in the previous year
- ☐ The impact of the previous year's expenditure (and evidence)
- ☐ Amount of PP allocation for current year
- ☐ Summary of the main barriers to outcomes for PP pupils at your school
- ☐ How you'll spend to address those barriers and why
- ☐ How you will measure the impact
- ☐ The date of the next review of your PP strategy.

PE and sport premium (primary only):

- ☐ How much funding your school received
- ☐ Details of how you spent the funding
- ☐ The impact on pupils' PE and sport participation and attainment
- ☐ How you'll make sure these improvements are sustainable
- ☐ The percentage of Year 6 pupils that can swim competently over a distance of at least 25 metres, use a range of strokes effectively, and perform safe self-rescue in different water-based situations.

Covid-19 catch-up premium (and/or summer school funding):

- ☐ How you plan to spend the grant
- ☐ How you'll assess the impact of the grant on attainment.

Careers programme:

☐ The name, email, and telephone of your careers lead

☐ Your careers programme including:

☐ Summary, including details of how anyone can access information about it

☐ Details of how your school measures and assesses the impact of it on pupils

☐ Date of your next review of the information.

Key stage 2 performance data (primary schools):

☐ Progress scores in reading, writing and maths

☐ Percentage of pupils achieving at least the expected standard in reading, writing and maths

☐ Percentage of pupils achieving a higher standard in reading, writing and maths

☐ Average scaled scores in reading and maths.

Key stage 4 performance data (secondary schools):

☐ Progress 8 score

☐ Attainment 8 score

☐ Percentage of pupils achieving a grade 5 or above in GCSE English and maths

☐ Percentage of pupils entering the English Baccalaureate (EBacc)

☐ EBacc average point score (APS)

☐ Percentage of pupils staying at school or going into employment after KS4.

Key stage 5 performance data (secondary schools):

☐ Progress

☐ Attainment

☐ English and maths progress

☐ Retention
☐ Destinations.

Governance information:

☐ Structure/responsibilities of the governing board and its committees, and full names of each chair
☐ Each active governor over the past 12 months:

☐ Full name
☐ Term of office
☐ Date of appointment
☐ Date if they stepped down
☐ Who appointed them
☐ Register of business and financial interests
☐ Governance roles in other schools/colleges
☐ Any interests arising from relationships between governors or between governors and school staff
☐ Attendance record at all meetings over the last academic year.

Extra bits for academies:

☐ If the school's owner is an individual, their name and telephone number
☐ If the owner is an organisation, their address and telephone number
☐ Details about your trust:

☐ Name of the academy trust
☐ Company number of the trust
☐ Registered office address of the trust
☐ Part of the UK where the trust is registered, e.g. 'England and Wales'

☐ The structure/responsibilities of the members, board of trustees and its committees and local governing bodies, and full names of each chair
☐ Current memorandum of association
☐ Articles of association

☐ Funding agreement

☐ Annual audited accounts (two years)

☐ Annual report

☐ Register of interests for the accounting officer

☐ Notice to improve (if applicable)

☐ The amount paid by the trust for someone's work who is not on the payroll, where it exceeds £100,000

☐ Number of employees whose benefits exceed £100k, in £10k bandings.

Extra bits for multi-academy trusts:

☐ Details of your trust's:

  ☐ Name

  ☐ Company number

  ☐ Registered office address

  ☐ Part of the UK you're registered, e.g. 'England and Wales'.

☐ The structure, remit, and full names of the chairs of:

  ☐ The members

  ☐ The board of trustees

  ☐ Committees

  ☐ Local governing bodies/academy committees.

☐ For each member who has served at any point over the past 12 months:

  ☐ Full name

  ☐ Date of appointment

  ☐ Date they stepped down (where applicable).

☐ For each trustee and local governor who has served at any point over the past 12 months:

  ☐ Full name

  ☐ Date of appointment

☐ Term of office

☐ Date they stepped down (where applicable)

☐ Details of who appointed them (in accordance with your articles).

☐ Each trustee's attendance records at board and committee meetings over the last academic year

☐ Each local governor's attendance records at local governing body meetings over the last academic year (if you have local governing bodies)

☐ Any relevant business and pecuniary interests, including governance roles in other educational institutions of members, trustees and governors

☐ The trust's scheme of delegation

☐ Master funding agreement

☐ Annual reports and accounts

☐ Articles of association

☐ Whistle-blowing policy

☐ All admissions arrangements

☐ Gender pay gap data

☐ Modern Slavery Act statement (if turnover >£36m).

Your governing body: things to consider

The 7 themes

The 7 themes are for you to use as an evidence base when discussing the performance of your school or trust, and the academies within it, with your board.

These come from the ESFA's 'Understanding your data: a guide for school governors and academy trustees' and provide a useful reminder of the aspects of school information and activity that you should be aware of and, where needed, challenging.

1. Pupil numbers/attendance and exclusions

Pupil numbers account for the vast bulk of your income. Understanding the growth or decline in numbers is vital to safeguard the financial health of your organisation. Look at recent trends, current numbers, and pupil number projections. This should include a breakdown to show first, second and third choices, and in-year churn in all year groups.

You should consider:

☐ Engaging with feeder schools.

☐ Transition from primary to secondary schools.

☐ Pupil projections/future financial planning.

☐ Differences between pupil projections and actual pupil numbers.

☐ Liaising with local authorities where required on pupil places.

☐ Pupil absence levels (including persistent absence).

☐ Absence levels by pupil characteristics including gender, ethnicity, first language, free school meals (FSM) eligibility, special educational needs and disabilities, long-term medical conditions, those who have needed a social worker/looked-after children (LAC), and children in need (CIN).

☐ Pupil moves (including exclusion levels).

☐ Suspensions and permanent exclusions.

2. Attainment and progress

Students' educational outcomes - remember, these will be different depending on the type and phase of your school.

So, at a high level, look at the breakdown of current data, by gender, free school meals, pupil premium, English as an additional language (EAL), special educational needs and disabilities (SEND), those with an education, health and care (EHC) plan, looked-after children, and so on.

Identify and then track/review any actions taken by staff to close the attainment gap and to improve year-on-year outcomes.

You should consider:

☐ The progress of students attracting pupil premium to the school.

☐ The progress of disadvantaged students by key stage/year group against that of their non-disadvantaged peers nationally.

☐ The use of pupil premium and how it is being used to raise the educational attainment of those targeted.

☐ The progress of students with an EHC plan or on SEN Support and an evaluation of the effectiveness of the provision made for them.

☐ The progress of students who have benefitted from the catch-up premium, tracked against the use of that funding.

☐ The published DfE performance measures:

- at KS2 - progress and attainment measures.
- at KS4 - Progress 8/Attainment 8 scores/English Baccalaureate (EBacc) measures.
- at KS5 - progress, attainment, progress in English and maths, and retention measures.

☐ The most recently published destination/career data for all students including those with SEND.

Some extra bits when considering the additional support for pupils with special educational needs or disabilities (SEND).

Things you might want to consider:

☐ Data on the SEND cohort in your school - compare the numbers of students identified with neighbouring schools, the LA, and national data.

☐ What percentage of the school population has SEND.

☐ What percentage has SEN Support.

☐ What percentage has an EHC plan.

☐ What is the breakdown of SEND by category of need?

☐ Spend and impact of funding spent on SEND.

☐ Is that funding targeted strategically based on your knowledge of the school SEND profile.

☐ Whether the SEN funding is leading to improved progress, and if so, how?

3. Curriculum planning: staff costs and class sizes

A bit of an overlap here, as having a grip on student numbers is key to effective financial planning. It will help establish a staffing structure that can deliver the greatest impact. The governing body/trust board should challenge their SLT on the effective organisation of the curriculum and the deployment of staff. (Note: all the acronyms shared here are covered in the dictionary section.)

Governors/trustees should look at factors including:

- ☐ Pupil-to-teacher ratio.
- ☐ Average class size.
- ☐ Teacher contact ratio (at secondary).
- ☐ Average teacher cost.
- ☐ Percentage of total spend on teaching/non-teaching staff.
- ☐ Percentage of total spend on senior leadership team.
- ☐ Spend per student for non-staff cost expenditure lines (for example, catering, ICT, energy, and curriculum supplies).
- ☐ Data on the deployment of teaching assistants (TAs and HLTAs).
- ☐ The amount of non-teaching time the special educational needs coordinator (SENCO) has available in relation to the number of pupils with SEN.

You should also consider:

- ☐ Whether the current deployment of staff resource supports the school's educational vision and student outcomes.
- ☐ Current and future student forecasts to identify any changes in staffing requirements, including consideration of any SENDs of current and future students.
- ☐ Progress over the school's published accessibility plan, which must include plans to increase access for disabled students to the curriculum.
- ☐ Where actual student numbers significantly deviate from forecasts.
- ☐ Succession planning/staff turnover.
- ☐ Any teaching and learning responsibilities (TLR) and increasingly any recruitment and retention payments.

4. Financial management and governance

All schools and academy trusts should have robust systems and processes in place to manage their finances securely and effectively, and provide assurance of this. It is important that board members understand the financial data that is presented to them to ensure there is sufficient challenge.

You should:

☐ Highlight any material differences/changes from your initial budgets and latest ongoing forecasts.

☐ Identify and challenge trends and inefficiencies to understand what is happening in your school/MAT.

☐ Track income versus planned and actual expenditure against budget forecasts, revenue expenditure and non-staff costs as a percentage of total expenditure (and of income).

☐ Check and be confident with your cash flow.

☐ Ensure student number projections have been accurate and if not, whether you re-budgeted accordingly.

There are several resources online to help you. Check out the '**School or trust's budget: financial benchmarking**' tool (www.gov.uk/guidance/schools-financial-efficiency-financial-benchmarking) and '**School resource management: checklist**' (www.gov.uk/guidance/school-resource-management-checklist). For MATs, the '**School resource management self-assessment checklist**' is also handy as it helps academy trusts check they are managing resources effectively and identify any adjustments they need to make (www.gov.uk/guidance/school-resource-management-self-assessment-checklist). Just to complete the set I'll also include here the **academy trust financial management good practice guides** (www.gov.uk/government/publications/academy-trust-financial-management-good-practice-guides).

Then we move on to a few considerations around school improvement activities and forward planning that all-important budget. The budgetary process should be embedded within the strategic leadership function. It is an integral part of the planning cycle, not an isolated activity.

With regard to active school initiatives, you should consider:

☐ Are school or academy trust improvement initiatives prioritised, costed, and linked to the budget?

☐ Are all new initiatives fully costed before the school or academy trust is committed to the proposal?

☐ Is there any additional workload burden to staff because of new initiatives?

☐ Do outcomes for pupils with SEND suggest you require a specific focus on SEND in terms of school improvement?

On the topic of ensuring we are working towards a clear three/five-year plan, I'd argue that if you can see beyond three years you must have a crystal ball given the turbulence in funding, but as a MAT you do need to submit three-year budget and cash flow forecasts to the ESFA under the label of a 'budget forecast return' (BFR). Within that context you should have considered:

☐ The school's formula funding for additional needs and the funding provided through pupil premium.

☐ Consulting the school's published pupil premium strategy and checking with your SLT about the rationale for the spending decisions and the impact on pupil progress.

☐ Planning for expenditure on your school buildings and infrastructure, including implementing your published accessibility plan.

With all this review of financial indicators, it's not a surprise to see a section on financial governance. The checklist is to ensure effective financial governance and committees have:

☐ Appropriate financial skills and the ability to understand and interpret data.

☐ Clear and concise monitoring reports of the school's budget position.

☐ Access to an adequate level of financial expertise from either the school business professional or finance specialist, including when those staff are absent (for example, on sick leave).

☐ Robust plans/policies/procedures in place to set, monitor and authorise spend and manage the risks of overspend.

☐ Adequate arrangements for audit of voluntary funds.

☐ Adequate arrangements in place to guard against fraud and theft by staff, contractors, and suppliers.

☐ A regularly maintained register of the business interests of boards and staff to avoid conflicts of interest.

Academy trusts must have an audit and risk committee to oversee and approve the trust's programme of internal scrutiny, and ensure risks are addressed and reported to the board on the adequacy of the trust's financial and non-financial controls and management of risks. They must include a report to the board on any non-compliance with the Academy Trust Handbook.

Finally in this section, you must ensure you have had a review of salaries, especially executive pay, as well as reporting (for MATs with >250 staff) on your gender pay gap.

5. Quality assurance

Trust boards/governing bodies should review their most recent Ofsted inspection report, taking note of any areas for improvement that are highlighted in the findings, alongside progress reports on action taken to address issues.

The Education Inspection Framework guide provides a detailed summary of the Education Inspection Framework (EIF) and can be found here: www.gov.uk/government/collections/education-inspection-framework.

In addition, trust boards should review any audit feedback as part of their annual cycle and ensure regular oversight of the trust's risk register. (See 'Risk register' section.)

6. Safeguarding and wellbeing

We've covered it earlier on in the book so you know all schools and academies must comply with **Keeping Children Safe in Education** (KCSIE) and alongside that, the **Working Together to Safeguard Children** (WT) statutory guidance. The latter is something less relevant for governors in their day-to-day work, and relates to the guidance on inter-agency working to safeguard and promote the welfare of children. It is included in the reference section.

This means that trust boards/governing bodies need to ensure their schools have effective safeguarding policies and procedures in place to safeguard and promote the welfare of their students. These include:

☐ An effective child protection policy, which:

- describes procedures in accordance with government guidance.
- references any locally agreed multi-agency safeguarding arrangements put in place by the safeguarding partners.
- includes policies such as peer-on-peer abuse, online safety and serious violence, and is available publicly via the organisation's website.
- is both reviewed and updated annually so that it is kept up to date with safeguarding issues as they emerge and evolve, including lessons learned.

☐ A behaviour policy.

☐ A staff behaviour policy (code of conduct).

☐ A policy setting out arrangements for when a child goes missing from education.

You should also consider:

☐ The types of concern recorded including any subsequent action taken including referrals to children's services or other LA support to identify emerging trends and mitigate the risk of re-occurrence.

☐ The effect of the concern on students and the impact of intervention taken because of the concern.

☐ Complaints received from parents or others, including staff grievances.

☐ Relevant external sources such as local media and the Ofsted review of sexual abuse in schools and colleges.

☐ The behaviour sanctions record.

☐ Inviting regular student and parent feedback.

☐ Reviewing the staff safeguarding training plan, and arrangements for updating staff on changes to safeguarding and child protection matters.

☐ Ensuring regular audit checks are being carried out effectively on pre-employment checks.

☐ Regularly challenging data around DBS clearance on staff and monitoring of the single central record.

☐ Health and safety records – accidents, near misses, emergency planning and responses, etc.

We're on the home straight now – last but not least...

7. The school community: staff, students, parents, and the governing body

I'm going to say this is largely a common-sense section. When it comes to your staff you should be considering:

☐ Reasons for any high staff absence or turnover.

☐ Staff performance/objective setting and appraisals.

☐ Succession planning.

☐ Any skills shortages for teaching/non-teaching staff and the same at board level.

☐ Staff feedback to measure levels of satisfaction, staff surveys, and exit interview summary reports.

Alongside that, ensure the board captures student and parent views as well, through survey and focus groups.

An annual governance checklist

What should the annual to-do list look like for an effective governing body? Fortunately, I wrote an article on this topic for *Headteacher Update* magazine in July 2020 (www.headteacher-update. com) and it still stands on the review process, so I have summarised it below.

Like most things in life, governing bodies have an annual calendar – I like to think of it as the governing body rhythm of the year. Let's look at some of the things a school will need to consider to help its governing body enhance and support its operation, questions that governors will need to ask to best fulfil their roles, and some recommendations for school governance throughout the year.

Assembling your governing body

At the start of each academic year, whether at local governing body or trust level, there are lots of things that need to be planned and prepared to ensure we are doing our jobs to provide the best quality of governance possible.

A good starting point is an annual review of the composition of your school's current governing body to check whether you have the right people around the table. One of the ways to do this is to complete a governor skills matrix each year, which will highlight each governor's professional skills and experiences, as well as record their confidence around the role they need to perform.

Next is the legal side of things – ensuring your governors complete their pecuniary interest forms (a requirement) and making sure they have read the latest national policies, such as Keeping Children Safe in Education (DfE). This is something governors should confirm they have read each year.

It is good practice to make sure governors are reminded of the Nolan Principles (also known as The Seven Principles of Public Life) (1995) and to make sure that appropriate inductions are planned for any new members of the team.

Enabling good governance

In the broader picture of enabling good governance, there are three key strands that governors themselves need to consider.

1. **Values.** What do we believe in? Are we doing the right thing? Being open-minded? Being purposeful?

2. **Understanding.** What do I know? Do I understand the finance and risk considerations in a school? Do I understand compliance, culture and what the role of governance is?

3. **Practice.** Am I able to influence, enable and support? Can I help with problem solving? Can I advise and do I get involved in the planning and organising?

Setting out responsibilities

Governance at local school level is always shaped by (certainly in the case of MATs) your scheme of delegation. This sets out the responsibilities and where within the trust structure those responsibilities lie. If you are a local authority standalone school, then of course you will have your own summary in terms of the governing body's responsibilities and making sure you are meeting all legal obligations.

You will be thinking about whether you are going to assign selected governors as link governors to particular topics (e.g. health and safety or a specific strand in the curriculum) and that there are appropriate training schedules (e.g. safeguarding or accessibility) in place for all governors.

Also, if you require any governors to help with the recruitment of staff during the year, they will need to complete the relevant safeguarding for recruitment courses.

The school year begins

Once the school year starts in September, a priority for governors is to review the key stage 1 and 2 results for a primary school, or GCSE and post-16 results for a secondary. Those results, particularly in subjects that may not have performed as well as expected, will most likely shape the content for the first standards or curriculum meeting at a local governing body.

They will also dictate whether any 'deep dives' or reviews of action plans are needed for underperforming subjects. These action plans are important, as they will allow the checks and balances for the governing body through the year to see what is being done to influence areas of improvement.

Other checks throughout the year will include:

- Any updates on staffing and teaching.
- Reviewing the pupil premium plan for the year ahead and, if you are a primary school, the PE and sport premium.
- Tracking of pupil premium spend and, most importantly, recording and evidencing what it was spent on and how you are going to measure the impact of that ring-fenced money.

- Ensuring your school website is up-to-date and regularly reviewed to confirm it complies with Ofsted requirements for the information it makes available for parents (Ofsted, 2018).
- Evaluating digital strategy. Perhaps, after recent events, ensuring that, at either a school or a trust level, a review of things like the school's digital strategy takes place, noting what worked and what did not work during the Covid-19 lockdown and what is required to facilitate or mitigate in the future, so that the school can operate more efficiently.
- Reviewing attendance and exclusions. Certainly, if you have any permanent exclusions, as per the changes in legislation, you will want to make sure that the governing body is aware of any destinations of those individuals.
- Monitoring behaviour and SEND reports.
- Comprehensive tracking of school data – especially curriculum data – and how that aligns with your school development plan. This might involve your link governor if you are looking at topics that did not perform as hoped the previous year.
- Ensuring transparency of finances. For trusts, making sure that the chair of the trust or finance chair receives monthly statements on finances (again, new legislation) is key to ensure budget monitoring and providing an on-going review of whether the school is operational and has funds to perform its task. This is particularly relevant to the local governing body if you are a standalone local authority school.
- Considering staff wellbeing. Think about how staff wellbeing within the school is facilitated and tracked, and ensure questions are being asked of the head and senior leadership to ensure staff are looked after and that their wellbeing is considered.

Ofsted calling

To provide the key data and indicators about your school that Ofsted will want to see, consider developing a SOAP report (see school on a page). Do you know what your school strengths and weaknesses are? The areas for development? This kind of report documents all the headline data for your school to ensure you have a complete, accessible overview.

Questions, questions

Good governance is about being a source of challenge and support to the school's head and senior leadership team. Some refer to it as being a 'critical friend', as it is only by asking difficult questions and having those discussions that the school is enabled to find the best way forward.

There are so many questions from the governing body to be built into the year. Often, these are shaped individually, school-by-school, based on the areas of development being focused on. Some typical ones are:

QUICK CHECKLIST

- ☐ How have you evidenced impact? How have you provided challenge?
- ☐ If you are a primary, is there sequencing in your curriculum? How do the themes follow on and build skills as children progress?
- ☐ Do you have confidence in your forecast for exam results at the end of the year? How are you benchmarking? How are you tracking and building that confidence?
- ☐ What about community engagement? As a governing body and as a school, how do you know that you are engaging successfully with your community and parents? And how are you developing that?

Once these basics are built into the annual rhythm of the governing body, then it really comes down to developing this, based on the challenges or strengths that your school is focused on.

What is most important is having your initial plan and making sure that, from the very first day, governors know what their obligations and responsibilities are for the year ahead. This way, when you reach the end of the year, you will be in the best position to perform a 360° review of the chair and the governing body's effectiveness – a reflective process that checks against the local governing body resolution or scheme of delegation to ensure all the tasks that are the responsibility of the local governing body have been addressed.

You can find the original article here: www.headteacher-update.com/best-practice-article/an-annual-checklist-for-your-schools-governing-body/228662/

Using A Competency Framework for Governance

It's great having a full governing body, and let's assume you meet regularly and think you are doing a pretty good job. That doesn't sound unreasonable, does it? The next question that will need to be considered is how do you know you have the right skills and experience around the table?

Well, fortunately the Department for Education produced **A Competency Framework for Governance** (DfE, 2017), which gives you a handy breakdown/checklist so that you can effectively self-evaluate your board, and I have included the following sections (1a to 6b) from the framework for you to refer to.

'The framework begins with the basic principles and personal attributes which, alongside the commitment of time and energy to the role, underpin effective governance. Following on from this, the knowledge and skills required for effective governance are organised into those which are essential for everyone on the board; those which are required of the chair and those which at least someone on the board should have.' (DfE, 2017) We always keep our fingers crossed for a someone! Naturally the aim is that the knowledge and skills required for chairs build on and complement the skills of everyone on the board.

The framework is built around 16 different competencies, but conveniently they are grouped under the same six headings you will have (hopefully) seen in the Governance Handbook.

Principles and personal attributes

The framework states, 'The principles and personal attributes that individuals bring to the board are as important as their skills and knowledge. These qualities enable board members to use their skills and knowledge to function well as part of a team and make an active contribution to effective governance.' (DfE, 2017) You should also check out the 'Nolan Principles' for standards in public life which I cover in my definitions section at the back of the book. So be prepared, there are a lot of Cs coming up, but if you are involved in governance, you should be:

- √ **Committed** – Devoting the required time and energy to the role and ambitious to achieve best possible outcomes for young people. Prepared to give time, skills and knowledge to developing themselves and others in order to create highly effective governance.
- √ **Confident** – Of an independent mind, able to lead and contribute to courageous conversations, to express their opinion and to play an active role on the board.
- √ **Curious** – Possessing an enquiring mind and an analytical approach and understanding the value of meaningful questioning.
- √ **Challenging** – Providing appropriate challenge to the status quo, not taking information or data at face value, and always driving for improvement.
- √ **Collaborative** – Prepared to listen to and work in partnership with others and understanding the importance of building strong working relationships within the board and with executive leaders, staff, parents and carers, pupils/students, the local community and employers.
- √ **Critical** – Understanding the value of critical friendship which enables both challenge and support, and self-reflective, pursing learning and development opportunities to improve their own and whole board effectiveness.
- √ **Creative** – Able to challenge conventional wisdom and be open-minded about new approaches to problem-solving; recognising the value of innovation and creative thinking to organisational development and success. (DfE, 2017)

OK, so now let's work through those six features of effective governance and see how we can evaluate ourselves against them. For each section you will see a set of expectations of everyone on the board and some extras for the chair, so don't worry if you can't tick everything straight away.

1a – Setting direction
Why it's important: Effective boards provide confident, strategic leadership to their organisations; they lead by example and 'set the tone from the top'.

The knowledge and skills required for effectiveness in setting the strategic direction of the organisation, planning and prioritising, monitoring progress and managing change.

Everyone on the board

Knowledge

- key themes of national education policy and the local education context
- key features of effective governance
- the strategic priorities (and where appropriate, charitable objects) of their organisation
- tools and techniques for strategic planning
- principles of effective change management
- the difference between strategic and operational decisions

Skills and effective behaviours

- can think strategically and contributes to the development of the organisation's strategy
- can articulate the organisation's strategic priorities (and where appropriate, charitable objects) and explain how these inform goals
- can put in place plans for monitoring progress towards strategic goals
- supports strategic change having challenged as appropriate so that change is in the best interests of children, young people, and the organisation (and aligned with charitable objects, where appropriate)
- is able to champion the reasons for, and benefits of, change to all stakeholders

---

The chair

Knowledge

- national and regional educational priorities and the implications of these for the board and the organisation
- leadership and management processes and tools that support organisational change

Skills and effective behaviours

- thinks strategically about the future direction of the organisation and identifies the steps needed to achieve goals
- leads the board and executive leaders in ensuring operational decisions contribute to strategic priorities
- adopts and strategically leads a systematic approach to change management, that is clear, manageable and timely
- provides effective leadership of organisational change even when this is difficult

---

1b - Cultures, values and ethos

The knowledge and skills required to set the culture, values, and ethos of the organisation successfully; demonstrate these in the conduct and operation of the board; embed them through the whole organisation; and monitor the impact on outcomes for children and young people and on the reputation of the organisation in the wider community.

Everyone on the board

Knowledge

- the values of the organisation and how these are reflected in strategy and improvement plans
- the ethos of the organisation and, where appropriate, that of the foundation trust including in relation to any religious character
- the code of conduct for the board and how this embodies the culture, values and ethos of the organisation

Skills and effective behaviours

- Can set and agree the distinctive characteristics and culture of the organisation or, in schools with a religious designation, preserve and develop the distinctive character set out in the organisation's trust deed
- acts in a way that exemplifies and reinforces the organisation's culture, values and ethos
- ensures that policy and practice align with the organisation's culture, values and ethos

The chair

Skills and effective behaviours

- is able to recognise when the board or an individual member is not behaving as expected and take appropriate action to address this
- leads board meetings in a way which embodies the culture, values and ethos of the organisation

---

1c - Decision-making

I could tell you I couldn't decide if I was going to include this section, but naturally my decision-making skills are exemplary (honest), and it should not be a surprise to you that...

Boards which operate effectively as strategic decision-makers are able to provide the foundation for creativity, innovation, and improvement in the organisation.

Effective decision-making is about moving from open and transparent discussion to achieving specific, measurable actions.

Everyone on the board

Skills and effective behaviours

- identifies viable options and those most likely to achieve the organisation's goals and objectives

- puts aside vested or personal interests to make decisions that are in the best interests of all pupils/students

- acts with honesty, frankness and objectivity taking decisions impartially, fairly and on merit using the best evidence and without discrimination or bias

- brings integrity, and considers a range of perspectives and diverse ways of thinking to challenge the status quo, rejects assumptions and take[s] nothing for granted

- identifies when to seek the advice of an independent clerk/governance professional for guidance on statutory and legal responsibilities and ethical aspects of the board's decision-making

- abides by the principle of collective-decision making and stands by the decisions of the board, even where their own view differs

- encourages transparency in decision making and is willingly answerable to, and open to challenge from, those with an interest in decisions made

The chair

Skills and effective behaviours

- ensures the board understands the scope of issues in question and is clear about decisions they need to make

- summarises the position in order to support the board to reach consensus where there are diverging views

- ensures that different perspectives, viewpoints and dissenting voices are properly taken into account and recorded

- facilitates decision-making even if difficult and manages the expectations of executive leaders when doing so

- recognises the limits of any discretionary chair's powers and uses them under due guidance and consideration and with a view to limiting such use

- ensures the board seeks guidance from executive leaders or others in the senior leadership team and from the clerk/governance professional before the board commits to significant or controversial courses of action

1d - Collaborative working with stakeholders and partners

Effective boards are well-informed about, and respond to, the views and needs of key stakeholders, particularly parents and carers. They enable productive relationships, creating a sense of trust and shared ownership of the organisation's strategy, vision and overall performance.

Everyone on the board
Knowledge
• key stakeholders and their relationship with the organisation
• principles of effective stakeholder management
• tools and techniques for stakeholder engagement, particularly with regard to engaging parents and carers
Skills and effective behaviours
• is proactive in consulting, and responding to, the views of a wide group of stakeholders when planning and making decisions
• anticipates, prepares for and welcome[s] stakeholder questions and ensures that these are answered in a relevant, appropriate and timely manner
• works in partnership with outside bodies where this will contribute to achieving the goals of the organisation
• uses clear language and messaging to communicate to parents and carers, pupils/ students, staff and the local community
• is credible, open, honest and appropriate when communicating with stakeholders and partners including clear and timely feedback on how their views have been taken into account
• considers the impact of the board's decisions and the effect they will have on the key stakeholder groups and especially parents and carers and the local community
• acts as an ambassador for the organisation
• supports and challenges leaders to raise aspiration and community cohesion both within the wider community and with local employers
The chair
Knowledge
• the links that the organisation needs to make with the wider community
• the impact and influence that a leader in the community has particularly on educational issues
Skills and effective behaviours
• communicates clearly with colleagues, parents and carers, partners and other agencies and checks that their message has been heard and understood

139

- consider[s] how to tailor their communications style in order to build rapport and confidence with stakeholders
- is proactive in seeking and maximising opportunities for partnership working where these are conducive to achieving the agreed strategic goals
- is proactive in sharing good practice and lessons learned where these can benefit others and the organisation
- demonstrates how stakeholder concerns and questions have shaped board discussions if not necessarily the final decision
- when appropriate, seeks external professional advice, knowing where this advice is available from and how to go about requesting it

1e - Risk management

I'd argue this aspect has never been more important than now, with a broad range of risks from retention of staff to sufficient funding and budget viability, to external pressures with costs rising, cyber-attacks and so much more.

Effective boards play a key role in setting and managing risk appetite and tolerance. They can ensure that risks are aligned with strategic priorities and improvement plans and intervention strategies provide a robust framework for risk management. These competencies enable those on the board to identify, evaluating and prioritise organisational risks and ensure appropriate action is taken to mitigate against them.

Everyone on the board
Knowledge
• the principles of risk management and how these apply to education and the organisation
• the process for risk management in the organisation and especially how and when risks are escalated through the organisation for action
• the risks or issues that can arise from conflicts of interest or a breach of confidentiality
Skills and effective behaviours
• is able to identify and prioritise the organisational and key risks, their impact and appropriate countermeasures, contingencies and risk owners
• ensures risk management and internal control systems are robust enough to enable the organisation to deliver its strategy in the short- and long-term
• advises on how risks should be managed or mitigated to reduce the likelihood or impact of the risk and on how to achieve the right balance of risk

• ensures the risk management and internal control systems are monitored and reviewed and appropriate actions are taken
• actively avoids conflicts of interest or otherwise declares and manages them

The chair
Skills and effective behaviours
• leads the board and challenges leaders appropriately in setting risk appetite and tolerance
• ensures that the board has sight of, and understands, organisational risks and undertakes scrutiny of risk management plans
• leads by example to avoid, declare and manage conflicts of interest
• knows when the board needs external expert advice on risk management

The next section of the competency framework is focused on your accountability for both the educational standards and financial performance of the school. They are important because 'these are the competencies that the board needs in order to deliver its core functions of holding executive leaders to account for the educational and financial performance of the organisation.'

2a - Educational improvement

These competencies enable the board to know that the information that they are receiving about the educational performance of children and young people is accurate, to challenge appropriately where necessary and to hold leaders to account for improving outcomes for all young people.

Everyone on the board
Knowledge
• the importance and impact of high-quality teaching to improving outcomes and the systems, techniques and strategies used to measure teaching quality, pupil progress and attainment
• the importance of a broad and balanced curriculum
• the rationale for the chosen curriculum and how this both promotes the ethos of the organisation and meets the needs of the pupils/students
• the relevant national standards for the phase and type of education and how these are used for accountability and benchmarking
• the relevant statutory testing and assessment regime

- the purposes and principles of assessment outlined in the final report of the Commission on Assessment without Levels.
- the rationale behind the assessment system being used to monitor and measure pupil progress in the organisation
- the key principles, drivers and cycle of school improvement
- the relevant indicators for monitoring behaviour and safety including information about admissions, exclusions, behaviour incidents, bullying and complaints
- the role of behaviour in maintaining a safe environment and promoting learning

Skills and effective behaviours

- establishes clear expectations for executive leaders in relation to the process of educational improvement and intended outcomes
- defines the range and format of information and data they need in order to hold executive leaders to account
- seeks evidence from executive leaders to demonstrate the appropriateness and potential impact of proposed improvement initiatives
- questions the leaders on how the in-school assessment system in use effectively supports the attainment and progress of all pupils, including those with a Special Educational Need or Disability (SEND)

Someone on the board

Knowledge

- the requirements relating to the education of children with Special Educational Needs and Disabilities (SEND)
- the requirements relating to the safeguarding of children in education including the Prevent duty
- the duties and responsibilities in relation to health and safety in education

Skills and effective behaviours

- Is confident in their challenge to executive leaders on strategies for monitoring and improving the behaviour and safety of pupils/students

2b - Rigorous analysis of data

I've always maintained that data without context isn't information. Increasingly schools generate more and more data and it's key we have an understanding of what data represents, and its relevance (the context) so that it can be used to shape effective challenge.

Everyone on the board

Knowledge

- the DfE performance tables and school comparison tool
- RAISEOnline for school and pupil data
- the evidence bases that data is derived from e.g. pupil attainment and progress data and how it is collected, quality assured and monitored across the organisation
- the context of the school and in relation to other schools
- information about attendance and exclusions in the school, local area and nationally
- the importance of triangulating information about pupil progress and attainment with other evidence including information from, executive leaders (e.g. lesson observations, work scrutiny and learning walks), stakeholders including parents, pupils, staff) and external information (benchmarks, peer reviews, external experts)

Skills and effective behaviours

- analyses and interprets data in order to evaluate performance of groups of pupils/ students
- analyses and interprets progression and destination data to understand where young people are moving on to after leaving the organisation
- uses published data to understand better which areas of school performance need improvement and is able to identify any further data that is required
- questions leaders on whether they are collecting the right data to inform their assessment and challenges appropriately when data collection is not adding value.
- challenges senior leaders to ensure that the collection of assessment data is purposeful, efficient and valid.

Someone on the board

Skills and effective behaviours

- reviews and analyses a broad range of information and data to spot trends and patterns

The chair

Skills and effective behaviours

- works with the clerk, to ensure the right data is provided by executive leaders, which is accessible to board and open to scrutiny
- promotes the importance of data interrogation to hold executive leaders to account

2c - Financial frameworks and accountability

We all love the financial bit, don't we? I really do, but I appreciate it's a subject that some find hard to access. It's such an important topic at the moment - not least with real funding pressures - that ignorance won't be an acceptable defence if we drop the ball on this.

These are the skills, knowledge and behaviours which enable the board to ensure that the organisation is in a strong and sustainable financial position to achieve its strategic goals.

Everyone on the board

Knowledge

- the financial policies and procedures of the organisation, including its funding arrangements, funding streams and its mechanisms for ensuring financial accountability

- the organisation's internal control processes and how these are used to monitor spend and ensure propriety to secure value for public money

- the financial health and efficiency of the organisation and how this compares with similar organisations locally and nationally [think benchmarking]

Skills and effective behaviours

- has a basic understanding of financial management in order to ensure the integrity of financial information received by the board and to establish robust financial controls

- has confidence in the arrangements for the provision of accurate and timely financial information, and the financial systems used to generate such information

- interprets budget monitoring information and communicate this clearly to others

- participates in the school's self-evaluation of activities relating to financial performance, efficiency and control

- is rigorous in their questioning to understand whether enough is being done to drive financial efficiency and align budgets to priorities

Someone on the board

Knowledge

- the organisations' current financial health and efficiency and how this compares with similar organisations both locally and nationally

Skills and effective behaviours

- uses their detailed financial knowledge and experience, which is appropriate for the scale of the organisation, to provide advice and guidance to the board

---

The chair

Skills and effective behaviours

- ensures the board holds executive leaders to account for financial and business management, as much as educational outcomes

- leads the board to identify when specialist skills and experience in audit, fraud or human resources is required either to undertake a specific task or more regularly to lead committees of the board

2d - Financial management and monitoring

After the financial frameworks come the skills to ensure that the board can make sufficiently informed and effective decisions on the use of resources and allocation of funds to improve outcomes. It is public money, and we need to show it has been used wisely.

Everyone on the board

Knowledge

- the organisation's process for resource allocation and the importance of focussing allocations on impact and outcomes

- the importance of setting and agreeing a viable financial strategy and plan which ensure sustainability and solvency

- how the organisation receives funding through the pupil premium and other grants e.g. primary sport funding, how these are spent and how spending has an impact on pupil outcomes

- the budget setting, audit requirements and timescales for the organisation and checks that they are followed

- the principles of budget management and how these are used in the organisation

Skills and effective behaviours

- assimilates the financial implications of organisational priorities and use this knowledge to make decisions about allocating current and future funding

- interprets financial data and asks informed questions about income, expenditure and resource allocation and alignment with the strategic plan priorities

---

2e - Staff and performance management

We all know there are huge pressures on our staff and bigger challenges with effective retention of our workforce. This section of the framework highlights the areas 'required by the board to oversee executive leaders in their responsibility to ensure that the organisation has the right staff who are managed and incentivised to perform to the best of their abilities'.

Everyone on the board

Knowledge

- the organisation's annual expenditure on staff and resource and any data against which this can be benchmarked against [sic]

- how staff are recruited to the organisation and how this compares to good recruitment and retention practice

- how staff performance management is used throughout the organisation in line with strategic goals and priorities and how this links to the criteria for staff pay progression, objective setting and development planning

- the remuneration system for staff across the organisation

Skills and effective behaviours

- ensures that the staffing and leadership structures are fit for purpose

- takes full responsibility for maintaining, updating and implementing a robust and considered pay policy

- feels confident in approving and applying the system for performance management of executive leaders

- identifies and considers the budgetary implication of pay decisions and considers these in the context of the spending plan

- pays due regard to ensuring that leaders and teachers are able to have a satisfactory work life balance

Someone on the board

Knowledge

- human resource (HR) education policy and the organisation's processes in relation to teachers' pay and conditions and the role of governance in staffing reviews, restructuring and due diligence

Skills and effective behaviours

- monitors the outcome of pay decisions, including the extent to which different groups of teachers may progress at different rates and checks processes operate fairly

The chair

Knowledge

- the process and documentation needed to make decisions related to leadership appraisal

Skills and effective behaviours

- is confident and prepared in undertaking leadership appraisal

- can explain to the board their proposals on leadership pay awards for approval

2f - External accountability

The final part of section 2 is about 'managing the organisation's relationship with those who have a formal or informal role in holding it to account'. Think Ofsted, ESFA, DfE, RSC, etc.

Everyone on the board
Knowledge
• the purpose, nature and processes of formal accountability and scrutiny (e.g. DfE, Ofsted, EFA etc.) and what is required by way of evidence
• the national performance measures used to monitor and report performance – including the minimum standards that trigger eligibility for intervention
Skills and effective behaviours
• ensures appropriate structures, processes and professional development are in place to support the demands of internal and external scrutiny
• values the ownership that parents and carers and other stakeholders feel about 'their school' and ensures that the board makes itself accessible and answerable to them
• uses an understanding of relevant data and information to present verbal and written responses to external scrutiny (e.g. inspectors/RSCs/EFA)

The chair
Skills and effective behaviours
• is confident in providing strategic leadership to the board during periods of scrutiny
• ensures the board is aware of, and prepared for, formal external scrutiny

3 - People

It hopefully won't come as a surprise to you, but governors 'need to form positive working relationships with their colleagues to function well as part of a team. They need to be able to relate to staff, pupils/students, parents and carers and the local community and connect to the wider education system to enable effective delivery of the organisations strategic priorities.'

This section covers the key strands around people.

3a - Building an effective team

These are the skills and behaviours necessary to ensure effective relationships and dynamics around the table. They help to foster a learning culture where constructive challenge is welcomed; thinking is diverse; a variety of experiences and perspectives are welcomed; and continuous improvement is the norm.

Everyone on the board

Skills and effective behaviours

- demonstrates commitment to their role and to active participation in governance
- ability to acquire the basic knowledge that they need to be effective in their role
- uses active listening effectively to build rapport and strong collaborative relationships
- welcomes constructive challenge and is respectful when challenging others
- provides timely feedback and is positive about receiving feedback in return
- seeks to resolve misunderstanding at the earliest stage in order to prevent conflict
- raises doubts and encourages the expression of differences of opinion
- is honest, reflective and self-critical about mistakes made and lessons learned
- influences others and builds consensus using persuasion and clear presentation of their views
- demonstrates professional ethics, values, and sound judgement
- recognises the importance of, and values the advice provided by, the clerk/governance professional role in supporting the board.

The chair

Knowledge

- the importance of succession planning to the ongoing effectiveness of both the board and the organisation

Skills and effective behaviours

- ensure that everyone understands why they have been recruited and what role they play in the governance structure
- ensures new people are helped to understand their non-executive leadership role, the role of the board and the vision and strategy of the organisation enabling them to make a full contribution
- sets high expectations for conduct and behaviour for all those in governance and is an exemplary role model in demonstrating these
- creates an atmosphere of open, honest discussion where it is safe to constructively challenge conventional wisdom
- creates a sense of inclusiveness where each member understands their individual contribution to the collective work of the board
- promotes and fosters a supportive working relationship between the: board, clerk/ governance professional, executive leaders, staff of the organisation and external stakeholders
- identifies and cultivates leadership within the board

- recognises individual and group achievements, not just in relation to the board but in the wider organisation
- takes a strategic view of the skills that the board needs, identifies gaps and takes action to ensure these are filled
- develop the competence of the vice-chair to act as chair should the need arise.
- builds a close, open and supportive working relationship with the vice-chair which respects the differences in their roles
- values the importance of the clerk/governance professional and their assistance in the coordination of leadership and governance requirements of the organisation
- listens to the clerk/governance professional and takes direction from them on issues of compliance and other matters

4 - Structures

Understanding and designing the structures through which governance takes place is vital to avoid unclear and overlapping responsibilities that can lead to dysfunctional or ineffective governance arrangements.

4a - Roles and responsibilities

Everyone on the board

Knowledge

- the role, responsibilities and accountabilities of the board, and its three core functions
- the strategic nature of the board's role and how this differs from the role of executive leaders and what is expected of each other
- In academy trusts, the role and powers of Members and how these relate to those of the board
- the governance structure of the organisation and particularly how governance functions are organised and delegated, including where decisions are made
- how the board and any committees (including local governing bodies in a MAT) are constituted

Skills and effective behaviours

- able to contribute to the design of governance and committee structures that are fit for purpose and appropriate to the scale and complexity of the organisation
- able to adapt existing committee structures as necessary in light of learning/ experience including evaluation of impact

<table>
<tr><td colspan="1" align="center">The chair</td></tr>
</table>

The chair
Knowledge
• the importance of their non-executive leadership role, not just in their current position but in terms of their contribution to local and, where appropriate, national educational improvement priorities
Skills and effective behaviours
• lead discussions and decisions about what functions to delegate

5 - Compliance

There seems to be an ever-increasing focus on this but this section of the framework is 'to ensure all those involved in governance understand the legal frameworks and context in which the organisation operates and all the requirements with which it must comply'.

5a - Statutory and contractual requirements

Everyone on the board
Knowledge
• the legal, regulatory and financial requirements on the board
• the need to have regard to any statutory guidance and government advice including the Governance Handbook
• the duties placed upon them under education and employment legislation, and, for academy trusts, the Academy Trust Handbook, and their funding agreement(s)
• the articles of association or instrument of government and where applicable, the Trust Deeds
• the Ofsted inspection/regulatory framework
• where applicable, denominational inspection carried in accordance with s.48 of the Education Act 2005
• the board's responsibilities regarding Equalities and Health and Safety legislation
• duties relating to safeguarding, including the Prevent Duty; duties related to special education needs and disabilities (SEND); and duties related to information, including in the Data Protection Act 1998 and the Freedom of Information Act 2000
• the school's whistleblowing policy and procedures and any responsibilities of the board within it
• the importance of adhering to organisation policies e.g. on parental complaints or staff discipline issues

Skills and effective behaviours

- is able to speak up when concerned about non-compliance where it has not been picked up by the board or where they feel it is not being taken seriously
- explain the board's legal responsibilities and accountabilities
- is able to identify when specialist advice may be required

The chair

Skills and effective behaviours

- sets sufficiently high expectations of the clerk/governance professional, as applicable, ensuring the board is compliant with the regulatory framework for governance and, where appropriate, Charity and Company Law
- ensures the board receives appropriate training or development where required on issues of compliance

6 - Evaluation

Well done for sticking through these; this is the last section from the competency framework.

Monitoring the board's effectiveness is a key element of good governance. The board needs to assess its effectiveness and efficiency and ensure ongoing compliance with its statutory and legal duties under review. Individuals should also reflect on their own contribution helping to create a stronger and more motivated board.

6a - Managing self-review and development

The skills and behaviours that help individuals on the board to reflect on how they personally are demonstrating the agreed values and culture of the organisation and what impact their individual contribution to making to [sic] effective governance.

Everyone on the board

Knowledge

- recognises their own strengths and areas for development and seeks support and training to improve knowledge and skills where necessary

Skills and effective behaviours

- is outward facing and focused on learning from others to improve practice
- maintains a personal development plan to improve his/her effectiveness and links this to the strategic aims of the organisation

- is open to taking-up opportunities, when appropriate, to attend training and any other opportunities to develop knowledge, skills and behaviours
- obtains feedback from a diverse range of colleagues and stakeholders to inform their own development
- undertakes self-review, reflecting on their personal contributions to the board, demonstrating and developing their commitment to improvement, identifying areas for development, and building on existing knowledge and skills

The chair
Skills and effective behaviours
• actively invites feedback on their own performance as chair
• puts the needs of the board and organisation ahead of their own personal ambition and is willing to step down or move on at the appropriate time

6b – Managing and developing the board's effectiveness

It is essential for the board to reflect on its own effectiveness including the effectiveness of its processes and structures. This will assist in building relationships and improving accountability and will enable the board to ensure that there is a clear distinction between strategic and operational leadership.

Everyone on the board
Skills and effective behaviours
• evaluates the impact of the board's decisions on pupil/student outcomes
• utilises inspection feedback fully to inform decisions about board development
• contributes to self-evaluation processes to identify strengths and areas for board development

The chair
Knowledge
• different leadership styles and applies these appropriately to enhance their personal effectiveness
Skills and effective behaviours
• sets challenging development goals and works effectively with the board to meet them
• leads performance review of the board and its committees
• undertakes open and honest conversations with board members about their performance and development needs, and if appropriate, commitment or tenure

- recognises and develops talent in board members and ensures they are provided with opportunities to realise their potential
- creates a culture in which board members are encouraged to take ownership of their own development
- promotes and facilitates coaching, development, mentoring and support for all members of the board
- is open to providing peer support to other chairs and takes opportunities to share good practice and learning

Amazing, well done. That's all six sections of the competency framework. Don't be overwhelmed by it, read it at your leisure, reflect on it section by section and dip into it when time allows. Not every measure will a be a yes/no answer. There will be some areas where you or your board feel less secure and that can be a good catalyst for a training session. Sometimes the best way to get up to speed is to ask one of your senior leaders who is confident in the area to do a short presentation at the start of a committee meeting covering the elements you think are still a bit grey.

Wellbeing: have you asked?

In case you weren't aware, the wellbeing of our children and staff has never been more important than right now. It is, after all, the foundation upon which almost all other aspects of school life are built. Post-pandemic we had lots of narrative around 'catch up' and 'learning loss' with some funding and interventions to support children getting back up to speed on their learning journeys, but ask any teacher and they will tell you first and foremost their efforts have been in supporting children with their social, emotional and mental health (SEMH) and, more broadly, the wellbeing of our children, so they are in the right space to re-engage with learning.

Throughout the pandemic and very much since, we have asked more and more of our staff in our schools and not always appreciated the impact this has had on their mental health. In fact, as governors, we have a duty to ensure our schools are doing all they can to support everyone's wellbeing, and it is part of our role to ensure all our staff, from the trust CEO down, are also being supported as best we can.

Dr Pooky Knightsmith is director of the 'Children, Young People and Schools' programme at the **Charlie Waller Memorial Trust** (www.charliewaller.org) and has been a governor at four schools. She is a highly respected and trusted voice on this subject and in an article for the National Governance Association (NGA) she shared some great advice for promoting positive mental health. You can find the full article here: www.nga.org.uk/Knowledge-Centre/Pupil-success-and-wellbeing/ Pupil-wellbeing/Mental-health/Promoting-positive-mental-health.aspx.

Alongside sharing advice on ensuring your policies and procedures in your school are relevant, accessible with lots of guidance on where to seek assistance, report concerns, and so on, she also includes some key questions governors should be asking. These include:

☐ Is our school a listening school?

☐ How aware is the school community of the importance of promoting good mental health?

☐ Do we have a mental health policy?

☐ Is mental health a part of our curriculum?

☐ Have staff been trained to recognise and respond to mental health issues?

☐ Do staff know who to refer mental health concerns on to?

☐ Have we usefully pooled our knowledge of local support and services?

☐ Have we considered how best to work with parents and the wider community?

☐ Are we meeting the emotional wellbeing needs of staff? (Knightsmith, 2019)

I think these are a really good way for you to ensure the conversation is started in your trustee or governing body meetings, and in the article she shares further tips for involving parents and staff as well as identifying if you are a 'listening' school.

Pooky also very kindly shared with me some top tips and advice to ensure you talk about mental health in your schools...

To get it really right, mental health needs to be a theme that runs through all of our governance work, rather than simply an add-on, because good mental (and physical) health is the bedrock on which all other activities within our setting are founded. When we get it right, it may go almost unnoticed. When we get it wrong, things start to fall apart.

It doesn't have to be a big job; we simply need to get used to bearing mental health in mind during our general governance work and being curious about which decisions and actions will help, rather than harm, wellbeing. Think about it like safeguarding; even when safeguarding isn't on the agenda, it's on the agenda because keeping children safe is at the heart of every decision we make and action we take. Promoting positive mental health is like an extended version of that, only it affects every member of your wider community, children and adults alike.

Mentally healthy schools are schools where:

- Happy, healthy children are more readily able to engage in learning and play.
- Staff recruitment and retention are positively affected. People will want to work with you and the risk of burnout and breakdown is reduced.
- Whole-school strategy is positively affected as happy, healthy adults are well engaged and able to make and follow through on decisions positively and confidently.
- Sickness, absence and presenteeism are reduced in both students and staff who are happier and healthier both physically and mentally (because mental health and physical health are deeply intertwined).
- Senior leaders are effective and engaged, and long-term absence is low. Succession planning is possible as staff are up for the challenge of taking on the responsibilities of more senior positions and haven't been scared off by stress and burnout, which can be endemic amongst senior leaders in less mentally healthy schools.
- Families choose your school above others for its positive, nurturing environment and great outcomes for students.

- You become more reachable for harder-to-reach communities, and engagement between school, home and the wider community improves.

Your time is limited and this book will have given you many other things to think about in addition to mental health, so here are the three top things I think are doable right away and which won't take up oodles of time but will be highly impactful:

1. **Appoint a named lead governor for mental health** – the key responsibility of this person is to always bear mental health and wellbeing in mind and to ensure that all policies, processes, decisions and actions are considered through the lens of mental health as well as the myriad of other lenses you're employing. Ideally, the lead governor should have a corresponding link person within the school staff such as the designated senior mental health lead or equivalent.

2. **Make the mental health of senior leaders a priority** – many schools I work with are doing wonderful things when it comes to promoting the wellbeing of their staff and students, but this is often led by one very burnt-out head or deputy. Make it your job to consider the mental health of those sitting at the top of the tree within your setting. Be a critical friend to them and encourage them to take the steps they need to ensure their own mental health so they can continue to do a great job looking out for everyone else.

3. **Be aware of burnout and proactively navigate crunch points** – there are certain points in the academic year that are notoriously challenging for staff and/or students. Points where we can barely drag ourselves out of bed and keep going, let alone give our best selves every day. That third week in November, the lead-up to mocks or exams and early February have been prime suspects in schools I've governed in England. Identifying and planning for the peaks and troughs in the mental health of staff and students can help to keep everyone happy and healthy and avoid burnout and absences. As a governing body, you're in a position to take strategic decisions that can have a big impact on the whole staff, as long as you plan ahead.

Start by identifying the 'low weeks' and then brainstorm whole-school approaches that could be taken to relieve the pressure in those weeks when everyone is most fragile, and give staff and students a chance to reset and refresh themselves instead. Ideas I've seen work well include:

- **A duvet week** – where there are no meetings or other commitments before school and everyone can get a little more shuteye.
- **A homework hiatus** – students get a break from homework and, consequently, staff get less marking for a few days.
- **Team teaching/off-timetable week** – by co-delivering lessons or having a special timetable for the week, the planning load can be reduced for staff. Even better if the week has a wellbeing/mental health focus for students. The planning of this kind of week can create additional work for some staff, but it can be planned ahead and what works well can often be adapted year on year.
- **Careful planning of your meeting calendar** – when looking at the year ahead, identify the low weeks and commit to keeping them meeting free. One meeting-free week a term can make the world of difference to a flagging staff body. As well as halting regular meetings for a few days, be careful to ensure that parents' evenings or other large commitments are scheduled outside of these times.

As a governing body, you'll likely have other ideas that might work well in your setting, so get imaginative. Small things will make a big difference if you lean into them.

Dr Pooky Knightsmith

The team at Governors for Schools also provide some useful guidance and questions including some around culture and practice, with questions like:

☐ What support is given to staff concerning their wellbeing? Is information readily available for staff and advice and guidance available for senior leadership? What training is provided?

- [ ] What do we do now to help staff to look after their own wellbeing?
- [ ] How do we praise and recognise staff performance?
- [ ] Do staff members communicate around wellbeing issues?
- [ ] What else could we be doing to make staff wellbeing part of the culture?
- [ ] How do we know what the current wellbeing of staff is like? How might we measure it? (Governors for Schools, 2021)

Remember to ask your senior leadership team how they are doing. They will be busy supporting their staff, but we need to make sure we don't forget about them as well. So, consider:

QUICK CHECKLIST

- [ ] How are our school leadership team ensuring that they have adequate support and are maintaining their own wellbeing at work?
- [ ] How can trustees/governors support this?
- [ ] Do senior leadership model positive working practices?
- [ ] Are you managing to maintain a reasonable balance?
- [ ] What approaches do other school/trust leaders take that we can perhaps consider employing in our organisation?

I am a big fan of the resources around wellbeing that are provided by the team at Persona Education (www.persona-life.com) for secondary school children (no, I'm not on commission). They have great resources for supporting social-emotional learning for teenagers. Given that student wellbeing is at the top of every school's agenda, and is now a priority for Ofsted, ISI, IB, CBSE and other frameworks, it's an area we should be aware of and we should be asking what interventions or tools our schools are putting in place. Tools like Persona (and to be fair, it's unique) empower non-specialist teachers to build student wellbeing and employability from age 13 to 19, improve academic performance and hit expected personal development targets.

Their approach builds student wellbeing and employability by developing 22 social-emotional life skills across six skill sets: being realistic, communication, open-mindedness, problem solving, resilience and self-control. I didn't even know there were 22 social and emotional life skills, but just to prove to you that they exist, the image below summarises them.

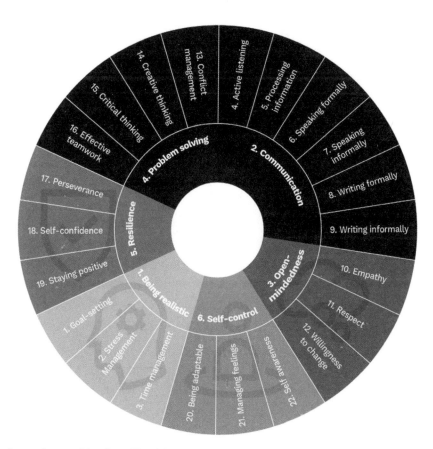

Source: Persona Education – 22 social and emotional life skills

There is a lot to consider around wellbeing, and it's handy to know there are resources out there to help, but the most important thing you can continue to do as a trustee or governor is to just ask 'How are you?', 'How are the team?', 'How are we supporting our cohort right now?' and 'Is there anything we can do to help?'

Digital: what are your plans?

Courtesy of the pandemic, you may have noticed that there have been a lot more conversations in your schools around the effective use of digital technology to support teaching and learning. In plenty of schools, that conversation has broadened to reflect on the role of technology in supporting both staff and student wellbeing, improving communication with parents (and the broader community) and how it can help free up time in the school day.

I appreciate that if educational technology (EdTech) is not your thing, this might sound like one topic that's worth skipping over, but please don't. The use of technology in our schools is nothing new and in fact the best examples are where we simply don't need to talk about them; they just do what they are intended for and are part of the fabric of our school. It doesn't matter if we are talking about the apps we use to teach maths, the tablets in the hands of our students, the Wi-Fi access points, our connection to online services, our central school management systems, or the interactive screen at the front of class – they all fall under this umbrella. So instead of only thinking about these as individual elements that you purchase when requested, think about what you have learned from other schools, listen to your teachers and students, and come up with a plan of where you could be in, say, five years from now. Most importantly, think about why any of the ideas you discuss are needed. Remember 'Mr Ofsted' and those key considerations: what's the intention, what's the implementation and how will we measure the impact?

I could really short-circuit this chapter and tell you that you need to read *My Secret #EdTech Diary*. It's written by a fab author (me 😊), and explains all things educational technology, past, present and future, in an easy-to-read, plain-English format. I have shared details at the back of this book, but I appreciate you didn't sit down to read my governance handbook only to be told to go and read a different one.

So, let's summarise our 'digital visions' and how we might plan a 'digital strategy'.

If we try to compile the main drivers for undertaking a digital strategy, the most common responses are:

- Looking for ways to enhance learning outcomes.
- Promoting student and staff digital wellbeing.
- Increasing attainment.
- Achieving better value for money (economies of scale).
- Developing collaborative technologies.
- Fostering stakeholder engagement/communication.
- Reviewing data security.
- Reading Al's *My Secret #EdTech Diary* (OK, I made this one up).

I am lucky enough to speak at educational conferences and events all around the world, and in my presentations I often start with a slide entitled 'Stop, Look and Listen', which really focuses our attention – reflecting on what we already have, where it is and if it's working well. You need to bring all the key voices within your school together, and before you dive into the 'what do we want' and 'why do we want it' conversation, consider a few key questions:

☐ How do we know what the current wellbeing of staff is like? How might we measure it?

☐ Do we have a clear analysis of what has worked well so far - what tools and technologies have proven to be a good investment and have become embedded and used on a consistent basis?

☐ Do we know where our collective digital skills lie - have we undertaken regular skills surveys to identify where our strengths and weaknesses are?

☐ Are we clear on the priorities within our school's development plan so that these can be aligned with our digital strategy?

As part of that review, it's important to have a digital inventory to hand - a clear picture of what tech we've got (types of IT devices, their location, their frequency of use, which applications are installed) and our infrastructure and its ability to flex with any change. It's vital that you collect data first, then assess before you plan.

In terms of a digital inventory, often an IT review will discover underutilised devices that can be deployed elsewhere for better efficiency, or software subscriptions that are being renewed on an annual basis but never actually used, or devices that are perfectly upgradable rather than automatically replaceable - and of course all these factors can help with short-term cost savings.

By this point we should have a good sense of what tech we have, whether it's being well utilised and what works well, and we can then start to get a sense of what we would like to achieve. To refine that plan and ensure we have the broadest set of voices aligned (bearing in mind that it's much easier to implement change if we have significant buy-in), the next step is to bring the stakeholder voices and views to the table.

Using a stereotypical and exaggerated example, for many schools the process of getting a decision on direction could be summarised as: business manager says there is some money available, someone asks for more of this item, item is bought and then the IT department are informed. There are so many opportunities for bad decisions in this process. The aim, of course, is to connect the dots - confirm that any solutions bought have the broadest possible impact and benefit, and that any decisions made are done so with an eye on the long-term aspirations - so that every investment has maximum value and is sustainable.

In terms of stakeholder voices, the first question needs to be: who gets a seat?

√ **Teachers and students** - they can feedback what works well, what doesn't, what they'd like to be able to do with technology in the classroom, what examples they've seen at other schools, advice shared from peers on their PLN, what tools they find most engaging and so on.

√ **Senior leadership team** - they will be able to review all the information shared, satisfy themselves that the priorities are being addressed, and they will feel consulted and informed so that they can make a judgement and sign off on any next steps.

√ **Network manager and IT team** - they can articulate their own priorities for digital infrastructure investment and ensure that any proposed solutions from other stakeholders will not be limited by or negatively impact the current IT infrastructure; and, as with every stakeholder, it's always better to be informed and know in advance what potential changes are coming their way.

√ **Data protection officer (DPO)** - to ensure any new approaches and solutions do not compromise or negate the school's data protection and data privacy obligations.

√ **Special educational needs and disabilities (SEND) team** - to share their current challenges and aspirations and ensure, where possible, every child can access the chosen learning solutions and, where it is not possible, that dedicated solutions to meet each child's needs are factored into the road map.

√ **Designated safeguarding lead (DSL)** - again, to share a view about any potential risks posed by, for example, developing our online resources or accessibility to technology, while also sharing any requirements they might have to further improve the school's e-safety solutions and promote digital citizenship.

√ **CPD lead** - to ensure that whenever the addition of new technology is discussed, the investment of time and budgets for suitable training is factored in to ensure the best possible chance of the technology becoming embedded, being used regularly, and having a tangible impact.

√ **School business manager or trust finance director** - to listen and understand the needs being articulated and once prioritised, identify the funds available and the pace that will be needed to move towards the ultimate goal. In other words, the money shouldn't dictate *what* happens, just *how quickly* it can happen.

√ **Trustees or school governors** – for oversight of any investment and to ensure constructive challenge of the conclusions reached.

√ **Parents** – important to be clear on what they find best supports their efforts in collaborating and working with the school and their children, and of course, what doesn't.

The above is a simplistic summary of the voices to involve and there will no doubt be others we can include, but it should be a good starting point to at least set the aspirations. As those ideas and requests are distilled down, we must also ensure that we remain focused on our overarching priorities, which should be shaped around pedagogy, alignment with the school development plan, being realistic within available capacity, having the best potential to be sustainable and reflecting on ways to measure and evidence impact.

What we are hoping to achieve can be encapsulated within these statements:

☐ A clear vision of what we are trying to achieve.

☐ An action plan of when, where, and how different things will be undertaken.

☐ A strategy to ensure staff are aware of who will be expected to use these technologies.

☐ An infrastructure in place to support these efforts.

☐ Training provided to ensure everyone knows how and when best to use technology and understands how it can support learning.

As Linda Parsons, digital superstar and my co-host on the **EdTech Shared** podcast (www.edtechshared.podbean.com), wrote: 'Don't start writing a Digital Strategy until you have tailored your school's Digital Vision! The vision you are about to write will stand as your guiding light for future applications of technology in your school, and also provide the solid foundation for all starting points of digital conversations' (Parsons, 2020).

So, your team have reflected, the voices of all the key stakeholders have been taken into consideration and you have some good ideas of what you want to achieve. It's quite possible someone has a new role or responsibility for digital technology in your school or trust, which is great, but you also need to ensure that there are bite-size areas of responsibility too, just so that it becomes more manageable. We chose in our trust to have some key pillars to focus our efforts around, which in turn allowed different staff to add value and take ownership of particular aspects. Our six pillars are below, but your school or MAT may of course have a different set of headings that works for them. I don't think there is a right or wrong here; it's all movement in the right direction after all.

As a governor or trustee, you should hopefully be invited into the conversation, especially if there are plans for investment in technology. Some early questions you might want to consider are along the lines of:

- ☐ Have we undertaken digital skills surveys with our staff, and are they being repeated so we can track confidence levels?
- ☐ Other than start-of-term INSET days, how often are our staff receiving CPD training on the key tools we use within our classrooms and how are we developing this?
- ☐ Are we capturing suggestions and feedback from teachers on what does and doesn't work?
- ☐ How will we capture ideas from new teachers who bring experiences from their previous schools?
- ☐ Does our senior leadership team have practical digital experience or a good understanding about how technology can be effectively used in the classroom?
- ☐ Do we have plans for (or a review of) a digital strategy and how can we help?

I would also encourage governors to be outward looking. When faced with challenges, it is very easy to become inward looking – responding to your specific set of challenges and needs, basing your planning on the capacity and skill set available. There is an opportunity to avoid unnecessary pitfalls or short-circuit the process if we are prepared to look outside our own schools and seek peer advice. Think again about the need to be outward looking when considering strategic plans. You might also want to ask a few broader questions – these are relevant for trustees to consider.

QUICK CHECKLIST

☐ Have we engaged with other schools or trusts to see how they have responded to recent challenges?

☐ How do our policies and approaches to governance compare to those of our neighbours?

☐ What worked best for other schools in our area in terms of online education delivery?

☐ Has anyone within our team engaged externally with other schools on their approaches to digital strategy?

☐ How could we benchmark and validate our effectiveness compared with our peers?

☐ If Ofsted (or equivalent) came to visit us tomorrow, would we have confidence articulating the decisions taken regarding our digital strategy and future plans for the delivery of any online learning, and would we be able to evidence its success as a result?

Remember, when it comes to the remote learning aspect, this isn't just something that would be nice to do. It's now an expectation in all schools that plans are in place for our digital capabilities and in particular our ability to deliver remote learning in the future. As a school governor or trustee, without a crystal ball in hand, you too would want to mitigate and future risks from another pandemic, and so it's not something we can deem irrelevant. The DfE have produced 'Providing

Remote Education: Guidance for Schools' (www.gov.uk/government/publications/ providing-remote-education-guidance-for-schools) which is worth checking out too.

Please make sure you think about EdTech. Think about not just remote learning to mitigate another pandemic, but for all the opportunities it might present to support teaching and learning, teacher workload, accessibility for learners and so much more. The workplace has changed; technology is a key skill that all our learners need to have confidence with, so where better than ensuring our schools are up to date and innovative with their use of technology.

If you would like to hear a high-level summary about taking your digital ambitions forwards for your school, then you can check out this **YouTube** video of a presentation I did in 2022 on the topic: https://youtu.be/kjRrkx19vLA.

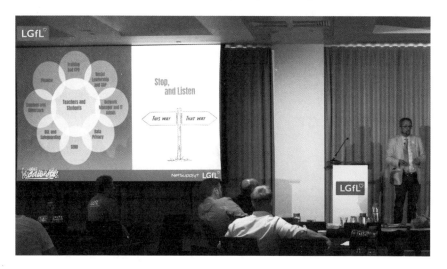

Risk register

As we know, risk is inherent in everything a school or academy trust does. It is a requirement within the Academy Trust Handbook that academy trusts manage risks to ensure their effective operation, and they must maintain a risk register.

A common approach is to consider risks under the following categories:

- Internal risks – these are the risks over which the academy trust has some control, by managing them through internal controls/additional mitigating actions. Some handy examples of these kinds of risks include health and safety risks and data security.
- External risks – these focus on big external events (I can think of one big one over the last few years) and consider how to make the trust more resilient to them. Recent examples include the response to the pandemic and dealing with extreme weather.

- Strategic risks – these are the risks to the delivery of the trust's core objectives. For example, common ones right now include loss of key staff, inability to recruit, academic outcomes, risk to reputation and so on.
- Project risks – these are the risks associated with any critical projects the trust may be involved in. For example, delays on the delivery timescale for a new building, not gaining sufficient student numbers to make a new school or expansion viable, etc.

You are encouraged to use the risk management framework to help shape your thinking.

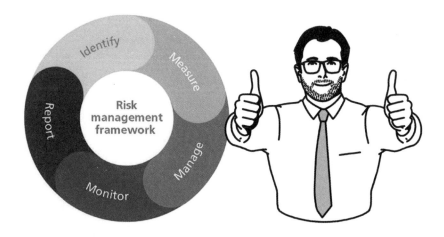

Once any kind of risk has been identified, it is important to quantify it so you can compare all risks identified consistently. Measurement typically consists of assessment, evaluation, and ranking. The aim of assessment is to better understand each instance of risk and how it could affect the trust. At a high level you should consider two key measures to score a risk:

- the **likelihood** (or probability) of it occurring, and
- the **impact** (or severity) if it did occur.

Give each of those measures a score of one to six (six being the highest risk) and multiply them together to get a risk score. You can then sort all your risks and see which have the biggest potential for impact. I could write lots more on this, but it would likely get a bit complicated, so the important thing to remember is that your risk index (your spreadsheet with all the risks identified) should be reviewed and updated regularly, and it should be brought to, and discussed at, your trust board on a regular basis.

This is a snapshot of how your risk register might look, and although it must be reviewed at least annually, I would strongly recommend it is a termly discussion. I'll start by summarising all the columns in your spreadsheet or equivalent, and of course this can be shaped to suit your trust's approach, so it is by no means a fixed format.

- **Risk number** - not sure I need to explain this one!
- **Risk description** - e.g. inability to recruit or retain staff.
- **Details** - the narrative around why this is a risk, e.g. local pressures and could have an impact on quality of teaching.
- **Existing actions** - what you currently do, e.g. HR procedures, exit interviews, staff support approaches, etc.
- **Source of assurance** - evidence to back up, e.g. details of your effective recruitment processes, regular staff surveys, etc.
- **Likelihood** - a scale of one to six with six being the highest, indicating how likely this risk is to happen.
- **Impact** - a scale of one to six again with six being the highest, indicating how significant this risk would be to the trust if it happened.
- **Risk score** - the likelihood multiplied by the impact - so a range of zero to 36. Then you can band scores - if you wish - into low, medium or high RAG (red, amber, green) ratings.
- **Planned actions** - steps you can or are taking to help mitigate.
- **Person responsible** - every risk needs an owner to monitor if the risk is increasing or decreasing.
- **Committee responsible** - which group of trustees will review this.
- **Progress update** - any information or details of actions taken since the last risk register review that are relevant to the discussion.

Those are all the key elements, although I would also encourage that while knowing a risk score is handy, a useful piece of additional context is knowing what the score was last time. Seeing an upward or downward trajectory is useful, so you might also want to include a column or two with the previous risk scores as a comparator.

I've seen some trusts opt for a really condensed version that looks like this:

No.	Potential risk	Likelihood	Impact	Risk score
1	GDPR breach	2	2	4
2	Pupil numbers fall	4	4	16

That table is followed by a mitigation summary, like this:

No.	Mitigation	New likelihood	New impact	Risk score
1	Enforce appropriate data controls	1	2	2
2	Attract academies/ reputation/quality teaching	2	4	8

The key bit is having a clear system for how you are reviewing, evaluating, and reporting these through your trust. The DfE guidance is clear and states:

'The board and the audit and risk committee should set out how and when it wants to receive information about risks. Information should be clear and provide key information on the significant business risks. The information should support the board and the audit and risk committee to assess whether decisions are being made within their risk appetite, to review the adequacy and effectiveness of internal controls, to re-prioritise resources and improve controls and to identify emerging risks.

'For this process to be effective it is important that the number of risks reported is appropriate to the trust's own circumstances and is a manageable number. If too many risks are reported the process may become more difficult to manage and may lose focus.' ESFA (2022)

See Academy Trust Risk Management for more details: www.gov.uk/government/
publications/academy-trust-financial-management-good-practice-guides/
academy-trust-risk-management

So, in terms of managing the risks once they have been evaluated and rated, you
need to be comfortable that you have appropriate plans in place to effectively
manage them. The approach you take will be linked in part to your own trust's risk
appetite and risk capacity; in other words, how much risk you are willing to take
and whether you have the people and capacity to manage them. The ESFA suggest
you use the 'four Ts' to assess your risk when factoring in the potential benefits
versus the costs, efforts, and disadvantages to your trust.

- **Tolerate** - to accept or retain the risk because you feel it's right to
  continue.
- **Treat** - to manage or reduce the risk with proposed interventions.
- **Transfer** - move the risk by contracting out or adding insurance cover, for
  example.
- **Terminate** - to stop what you are doing and eliminate the risk.

Finally, as part of Academy Trust Risk Management, the DfE provide some handy
reminders on common pitfalls.

- **Reporting too many risks**: trusts can fall into the trap of tracking too
  many risks or ones that substantially overlap. The board should clarify the
  number of risks they are able to oversee, maybe prioritising their 'top 10'.
- **Ignoring known risks**: risks are sometimes ignored because of
  organisational politics or the preferences of a dominant personality. Are
  you ignoring the elephant in the room because of the tone at the top? This
  is more common than you think.
- **Overreliance on subjective judgement**: one person's risk is another person's
  opportunity and individual perceptions influence the way risks are assessed.
  Potential risks should be discussed with the aim of reaching a common
  understanding of what they are and how they should be dealt with.
- **No real buy-in at a senior level**: the person who administers the risk
  management framework may not have the seniority to have an impact
  or the capacity to fulfil the role effectively. As a result, risk management

may not get the required attention and the process may decline into a tick-box exercise. The audit and risk committee role is to ensure the risk management framework in place is effective.

- **Risks not linked to strategic objectives**: commonly risks are captured from the bottom up and this can leave them disassociated from strategic objectives. Although ultimate responsibility for risk management lies with the board, everyone in the academy trust has a role to play in identifying risks to business goals.

- **Over-complexity**: endless discussions about methodology and terminology, which leave no time left to address the risks themselves, are symptomatic of an over-engineered approach. This is an easy trap to fall into but hopefully this chapter has helped simplify the process for you.

- **Not using the output**: organisations that put the review of risks as the last item on meeting agendas run the risk of an unexpected event having a significant negative impact. (ESFA, 2022)

Ofsted

OK, so I had to go and spoil all the positivity by creating a section on our friends at Ofsted. Sorry about that! On a slightly more serious note, don't lose sleep over them coming to visit your school. Your leadership team will potentially think of them as a bit of a 'sword of Damocles' hanging over the school when you are due a visit, but as with anything, control what you can control, and don't sweat over what you can't.

If you are entirely new to school governance, perhaps we need to take a couple of small steps backwards, just to explain who Ofsted are and what their role is, in a basic way.

Ofsted (or to use the full name, the Office for Standards in Education) is a non-ministerial department of the UK government, reporting to Parliament. Ofsted is responsible for inspecting a range of educational institutions, including state schools and some independent schools in England. In essence, they are responsible for ensuring our schools are operating safely and to high standards. It's not unreasonable to have someone check our children are at schools that are performing well. The concept is reasonable, but from a number of personal encounters, the experience isn't always as collaborative as you would hope and it does sometimes feel like it's pot luck who you get on the inspection team and what they are trying to achieve. That's a polite way of saying many inspectors are great, but some seem to arrive with an agenda, looking for an issue and ignoring everything else. It's not a regular occurrence though. They typically visit schools every four years or so, potentially after two years if they have concerns about the school.

Anyway, I digress. When Ofsted come to your school for an inspection, at the end of the visit your school will receive a judgement which can be one of four ratings, of which you are hoping to get a one or two:

☐ Grade 1 - outstanding

☐ Grade 2 - good

☐ Grade 3 - requires improvement

☐ Grade 4 - inadequate.

They form this judgement based on the criteria defined in the Education Inspection Framework (www.gov.uk/government/publications/education-inspection-framework/education-inspection-framework). I'd encourage you to take a look yourself as it helps shape your understanding of the questions they might ask. Yes, that's right. As part of their inspection they will ask to meet with the chair of governors and possibly a couple of other governors who are available. I'll expand on that later. Let's start by just unpicking at a high level the categories the inspection framework is broken down into.

Quality of education

Under the 'quality of education' judgement category, the inspectors will look at the three Is of the Ofsted framework: intent, implementation and impact (DfE, 2022a).

Intent

✓ How your staff construct the curriculum and if it's designed to give all the necessary knowledge and cultural capital needed by all learners, including disadvantaged students, those with special needs, and those with disabilities and high needs.

✓ Learners are taught a full range of subjects for as long as possible, 'specialising only when necessary'.

Implementation

✓ Do all your teachers have a good knowledge of the subject they teach? Do they present their subject clearly? Do they check learners' understanding systematically and provide feedback, while also responding and adapting their teaching methods as needed?

✓ Can your teacher ensure that learners remember what they have been taught in the long term?

✓ Do the learning environment, the resources, and materials created and used by teachers support the planned curriculum in providing learners necessary knowledge and skills?

✓ Is there special importance placed on reading that is seen as an activity that can develop learners' confidence and their enjoyment of reading?

Impact

✓ Having acquired knowledge and skills through the curriculum, do learners achieve well? This is mostly reflected in the results of national tests and examinations.

✓ Do learners read 'widely and often, with fluency and comprehension'?

✓ Do learners gain qualifications that let them continue their course of study and enable them to move on to further education, employment or training?

They will also look at...

Behaviour and attitudes

To review, evaluate and judge behaviour and attitudes, inspectors will have discussions with students from different backgrounds as well as staff to collect information and evidence about the school culture and practice related to the field. Alongside that, they are encouraged to look for evidence that:

✓ There are high expectations in place regarding learners' behaviour, which are applied in a consistent and fair manner. This is also reflected in learners' behaviour.

✓ Learners have a positive attitude towards their education and are committed to learning, know how to study and take on challenges effectively, and are able to be proud of their achievements.

✓ The attendance of learners is high, and they are also punctual.

✓ The relationship between staff and learners is positive and respectful.

✓ In the environment, created by leadership, teachers and learners, 'bullying, peer-on-peer abuse or discrimination are not tolerated' and in case of any related situations, the staff handles them quickly and effectively.

Next up the framework focuses on...

Personal development

When looking at personal development the inspectors are looking to evaluate that:

✓ The curriculum, beyond serving purely academic goals, supports the broader development of learners, helping them find their interests and talents, and develop those interests and talents.

✓ The curriculum provides what is needed for learners to develop their character, and to stay physically and mentally healthy.

✓ The provider and educator prepare learners for future success and 'life in modern Britain'.

Within their judgement they are also looking for evidence that the school provides an effective careers programme with suitable and appropriate careers advice being offered to students. That should include what they identify as unbiased advice, an opportunity to get an experience of work, opportunity to have contact with employers and signposting future training opportunities.

Leadership and management

I left this one until last as this is the section where you as a governor get to be involved and contribute, albeit for a small part of the overall process. I always work on the basis that the school leadership team put so much effort into our schools, that during the inspection process as governors we don't want to undermine their efforts by not being able to have a positive and informed conversation with the inspector ourselves. The key areas from the framework that inspectors will be examining are below and you'll see governance at the bottom.

✓ Leaders and educators have strong, shared values, policies and practices in place, supporting a clear vision of how they plan to provide high-quality, inclusive education to all.

✓ Leaders and educators concentrate on the long-term development of staff, their subject and pedagogical knowledge, and appropriate use of assessment.

✓ Leaders and educators make sure that all learners complete their studies.

✓ Leaders can successfully engage with learners, staff, parents, carers, employers, local services; and they are constructive and helpful in a realistic manner when managing staff.

✓ Leaders protect their staff from bullying and harassment.

✓ **'Those responsible for governance'** ensure that the provider has a clear strategy with well-managed resources, and hold them accountable for fulfilling their duties, for example, with regards to safeguarding.

So as this is a governance handbook, what should we make sure we do to ensure we get a nice big 'tick' in the inspector's box? Here is a quick checklist to hopefully make it easy to navigate.

☐ **Understand what the role of a school governor is and your responsibilities.**

Review the Governance Handbook (www.gov.uk/government/publications/ governance-handbook) and A Competency Framework for Governance.

☐ **Have a good working knowledge of your school.**

Think about the school context and how it performs compared to others. Know your key policies and what your school priorities are alongside performance data for key groups (see 'school on a page' later in the book).

☐ **Ensure you can demonstrate evidence of governor challenge.**

Make sure your minutes are in good order. It helps to highlight in them where questions and challenges were made during the meeting. Show any records of governor visits, reviews, link meetings and so on.

☐ **Evidence steps taken to keep staff and students safe in school.**

Show evidence that all governors have read KCSIE and the Prevent duty, ideally that you have a nominated link governor for safeguarding, that you have done a safeguarding audit, and so on.

☐ **Show that you have seen your school's self-evaluation form (SEF) and school improvement plan (SIP).**

Governors should be able to discuss how they monitor this in curriculum/standards meetings, understand and explain why each priority has been identified, know what progress has been made to date and if there are any future plans in place. I think this is the most important area where governors should be able to speak confidently on the subject matter.

☐ **Prep yourself and have a read of the Education Inspection Framework (EIF).**

It's always good to have a clear understanding of what to expect during an inspection. I have summaries for you here but if you want to read in detail then head to the link I shared at the start of this section.

☐ **Know what progress your school has made since its last inspection.**

The advice given is that governors should be able to talk about any progress they have made since their last inspection. Unsurprisingly, inspectors will be looking for this. It is equally important to be comfortable and confident about what hasn't happened yet, and reassure them there are plans to address this as soon as possible.

☐ **Check those policies.**

Sounds obvious, but it's really important all your policies are up to date and clearly published on your school website.

☐ **Make sure your school website is compliant.**

Don't worry, there is a section and checklist on this included in the book.

☐ **Show them the evidence.**

For any key areas you expect the inspectors to focus on, where appropriate, bring evidence with you to the meeting – perhaps survey results, deep dive meetings you have had, planning evidence... Every little helps. 😉

And just to cap off this section, if you do join a meeting with an inspector, expect questions like this to pop up.

- Are your students making good progress? How do you know?
- What are your school's main areas for development?
- What are your school's main strengths and weaknesses?
- What is the current quality of teaching and learning in the school? How do you know?
- Is the quality of teaching the same throughout the school? How do you know?
- What do you know about CPD of your staff? What is the impact of CPD? How do you know?
- How much is your pupil premium this year and how well is it being used?
- What can you tell me about how pupil premium is spent?
- What is the behaviour of students like in your school?
- Do you know how poor behaviour is addressed?
- Do children feel safe in your school? How do you know?
- What do your parents think of your behaviour policy? How do you know?
- How do you support your head in their role?
- How do you monitor performance management for your head?
- How do you know safeguarding is effective in your school?
- How are your SEND cohort doing compared to others and how do you monitor this?
- Which groups of your children are making the least progress? How are you addressing this?

I could keep writing example questions for pages, but hopefully that gives you a flavour of what you might be asked. So remember, if you are comfortable that you know what you need to know, then don't worry. The inspector is there to hear that you are doing the right things, and not there to try to catch you out.

School on a page (SOAP) report

No, it's not an opportunity to 'clean things up'; SOAP is a school on a page summary that gives leaders a clear oversight on all key data and a handy reference point over time.

For many governors it's a really useful tool should you get a call from Ofsted and need to ensure everyone is on the same page with their data. It's not nice having to prep and check the night before.

I have included a few bullet points below that may be a useful starting point when discussing with your school leaders.

Key information contained in a SOAP report might be:

- School context
- Attendance
- School objectives for the year (linked to the school development plan)
- The school's SEF (self-evaluation form)
- The school's data showing high-level results for all key indicators
- Comparisons with either regional or national averages

- Pupil and sports premium summary
- Next steps/priorities (again, linked to the school's development plan)
- Successes/areas to highlight and celebrate
- Key areas for development
- A post-16 destinations summary
- Highlights from parent surveys.

Annual calendar: academies financial planning

Our friends at the Education and Skills Funding agency (ESFA) and the Department for Education (DfE) have lots of points in the year when they want information from us or send things to us. Their guide 'Academies Planning Calendar' is a handy summary of key dates and actions related to academy funding, finance, and your MAT compliance within your funding agreement.

There is quite a lot to it, but I always think it's helpful to take a quick look at the upcoming month and see if there is anything that the trust should be doing that you or your committee haven't heard about yet. You can find the latest version here – www.gov.uk/government/publications/academies-planning-calendar – but below is a handy checklist which you can use each year.

September
Trust actions: • Academies must submit their public sector apprenticeship target data returns for the period 1 April to 31 March of the year just gone by 30 September.
Information and published guidance: • The latest version of the Academy Trust Handbook comes into effect.
Payments:

October

Trust actions:

- Complete your autumn school census.
- Land and buildings collection tool online form completed early October.
- Accounts return online form available middle of October.

Information and published guidance:

- ESFA publishes guidance and workbook for the academies accounts return.
- ESFA publishes accounts submission form for academies to submit their audited financial statements, auditor's management letter and annual summary internal scrutiny report.
- ESFA publishes the 16 to 19 revenue funding allocation data for the next year.
- Pupil number adjustment (PNA) calculator and guidance notes published for the next year.

Payments:

- Second quarterly pupil premium payment for new financial year.
- Universal infant free school meals (UIFSM) for newly eligible academies.
- First payment of the school-led tutoring grant and first payment of the recovery premium for the new academic year (may not be applicable post 2023).

November

Trust actions:

- Complete and submit the land and buildings collection tool by early November.

Information and published guidance:

- PE and sport premium conditions of grant and allocations issued for the next academic year.
- DfE publishes the prior year academies sector annual report and accounts (SARA).

Payments:

- First payment of the teachers' pay grant and teachers' pension grant for the new academic year (early years and post-16 providers only).
- First PE and sport premium payment for the new academic year.
- Reimbursement of approved summer schools programme claims for the previous summer.

December

Trust actions:

- Trusts submit their prior year audited financial statements, auditor's management letter, annual summary internal scrutiny report and accounts submission coversheet by 31 December.

Information and published guidance:

- DfE announces the school's revenue funding settlement for the current financial year.

Payments:

January

Trust actions:

- Complete spring school census.
- Schools resource management self-assessment tool (SRMSAT) online form available.
- Complete and submit the accounts return online form by late January.
- Trusts publish their prior year audited financial statements on their website by 31 January.

Information and published guidance:

- ESFA publishes outcomes of requests from local authorities for changes to high needs places for the current financial year; academies have two weeks to submit a query about the outcomes.
- ESFA issues guidance on estimating your funding for April to August openers in the next financial year.

Payments:

- Third quarterly pupil premium for the current financial year.
- Second payment of the recovery premium for the current financial year.
- Second payment of the school-led tutoring grant.

February
Trust actions:
• Academies must determine their admission arrangements for entry in September of the next full year by the end of February. So, if you are reading this in 2023, it's for entries in September 2024.
• Academies must publish their admissions appeals timetable for next year on their website by 28 February.
Information and published guidance:
• ESFA confirms exceptional current year post-16 in-year growth outcomes.
• ESFA issues guidance on next year's funding allocations for open academies.
• ESFA issues guidance on funding allocations for new openers between April and August next year.
• ESFA issues 16 to 19 allocation calculation toolkits (ACT) containing funding factors and student numbers.
Payments:
• Positive early PNA payments made to academies for current financial year.

March
Trust actions:
• Academies must publish their admission arrangements for entry in September of the next year on their website and send a copy to their local authority by mid-March.
• Trusts complete and submit the school resource management self-assessment tool (SRMSAT) by mid-March.
Information and published guidance:
• ESFA issues academy revenue funding allocations for current year including 16 to 19 allocations (plus student support, 16 to 19 Bursary Fund and free meals in further education) where applicable.
• ESFA publishes the Academies Accounts Direction, Model Accounts and Auditor Guide for current year.
Payments:
• PE and sport premium for newly eligible academies.

April

Trust actions:

- 16 to 19 revenue funding allocation business case for major data errors deadline end of April.

Information and published guidance:

- ESFA publishes 16 to 19 funding regulations guidance, funding rates and formula guidance for current financial year.
- ESFA publishes 16 to 19 student support eligibility and guidance, including 16 to 19 Bursary Fund guidance.
- ESFA publishes guidance and workbook for the budget forecast return.

Payments:

- Final quarterly pupil premium for the current financial year.
- Third payment of the recovery premium for the current academic year.

May

Trust actions:

- Complete summer school census.
- Trusts must submit their audited financial statements to Companies House within nine months of the end of the accounting period which is 31 May.

Information and published guidance:

- Main PNA (pupil number adjustment) exercise complete and statements uploaded to Document Exchange for current academic year.

Payments:

- Second payment of the teachers' pay grant and teachers' pension grant for the current academic year (early years and post-16 providers only).
- Final PE and sport premium for the current academic year.
- Final payment of the school-led tutoring grant for the current academic year.

June

Trust actions:

- Budget forecast return form (BFR) available.

Information and published guidance:

- ESFA publishes the Academy Trust Handbook for the next academic year.
- ESFA publishes the 16 to 19 subcontracting controls guidance for current year.
- ESFA issues guidance on funding allocations for new openers between September of this year and March of next year.

Payments:

July

Trust actions:

- Complete and submit the budget forecast return.

Information and published guidance:

- ESFA refreshes the 16 to 19 interactive census tool.
- DfE publishes last academic year's academies sector annual report and accounts (SARA).
- ESFA issues guidance on estimating your funding, for schools opening in the next academic year.

Payments:

- Final payment for universal infant free school meals for the current academic year.
- Quarter 1 payment of pupil premium.
- Main PNA positive payments made to academies.
- Final payment of the recovery premium for the current academic year.

August

Breathe and plan to do it all over again next year. ☺

Handy resources

Academy Trust Handbook – www.gov.uk/government/publications/academies-financial-handbook

Academies Planning Calendar – www.gov.uk/government/publications/academies-planning-calendar

Academy and free school funding agreement: multi-academy master – www.gov.uk/government/publications/academy-and-free-school-multi-model-master-funding-agreement

Academy trust financial management good practice guides – www.gov.uk/government/publications/academy-trust-financial-management-good-practice-guides

Al Kingsley's blog – www.alkingsley.com

'An annual checklist for your school's governing body', Headteacher Update, July 2020 – www.headteacher-update.com/best-practice-article/an-annual-checklist-for-your-schools-governing-body/228662/

BESA (British Educational Suppliers Association) – www.besa.org.uk

CCMS, Council for Catholic Maintained Schools – https://www.ccmsschools.com

Charlie Waller Trust – www.charliewaller.org

Child Exploitation and Online Protection (CEOP) – www.ceop.police.uk/Safety-Centre

Children Missing Education – www.gov.uk/government/publications/children-missing-education

Classroom.cloud (teaching and online safety) - www.classroom.cloud

Constitution of governing bodies of maintained schools - www.gov.uk/government/publications/constitution-of-governing-bodies-of-maintained-schools

Data protection: toolkit for schools (DfE) - www.gov.uk/government/publications/data-protection-toolkit-for-schools

Designated teacher for looked-after and previously looked-after children - www.gov.uk/government/publications/designated-teacher-for-looked-after-children

Digital Citizenship Institute - www.digcitinstitute.com

EdTech Shared Podcast - https://edtechshared.podbean.com

Forbes Technology Council - www.forbes.com

Foundation for Education Development - www.fed.education

GBA - Governing Bodies Association Northern Ireland - www.gbani.org

Governance Handbook - www.gov.uk/government/publications/governance-handbook

GovernorHub - www.GovernorHub.com

Governors for Schools - www.governorsforschools.org.uk

Hampton Academies Trust - www.hamptonacademiestrust.org.uk

Headteacher Update magazine - www.headteacher-update.com

Information Commissioner's Office (ICO) - www.ico.org.uk

Internet Watch Foundation (IWF) - www.iwf.org.uk

Keeping Children Safe in Education (KCSIE) - www.gov.uk/government/publications/keeping-children-safe-in-education--2

Natterhub (DigCit resources) - www.natterhub.com

NetSupport (cool education software) - www.netsupportsoftware.com

NGA - National Governance Association - www.nga.org.uk

Persona Education (SEMH resources) - www.persona-life.com

'Promoting Positive Mental Health' Dr Pooky Knightsmith (NGA) - www.nga.org. uk/Knowledge-Centre/Pupil-success-and-wellbeing/Pupil-wellbeing/Mental-health/ Promoting-positive-mental-health.aspx

Providing remote education: guidance for schools - www.gov.uk/government/ publications/providing-remote-education-guidance-for-schools

School Admissions Code - www.gov.uk/government/publications/school-admissions-code--2

School governance update (DfE) - www.gov.uk/government/publications/school-governance-update

School resource management: checklist - www.gov.uk/guidance/school-resource-management-checklist

School resource management self-assessment checklist - www.gov.uk/guidance/ school-resource-management-self-assessment-checklist

School or trust's budget: financial benchmarking tool - www.gov.uk/guidance/ schools-financial-efficiency-financial-benchmarking

School performance tables - www.gov.uk/school-performance-tables

Schoolsweek magazine - www.schoolsweek.co.uk

SCIS, Scottish Council of Independent Schools - www.scis.org.uk

SecEd magazine - www.sec-ed.co.uk

SEND code of practice: 0 to 25 years - www.gov.uk/government/publications/send-code-of-practice-0-to-25

Statutory policies for schools - www.gov.uk/government/publications/statutory-policies-for-schools

Teaching Online Safety in Schools - www.gov.uk/government/publications/teaching-online-safety-in-schools

The Bett show - www.bettshow.com

The Hoot (governance news) - www.thehoot.news

The Key for School Governors (governance resources) - https://schoolgovernors.thekeysupport.com

The MAT Partnership Network (MATPN) - https://matpn-uk.com/

The Multi Academy Trust Association - www.matassociation.org

The School Trustee blog - www.schooltrustee.blog

The Schools and Academies Show - www.schoolsandacademiesshow.co.uk

Understanding your data: a guide for school governors and academy trustees (ESFA) - www.gov.uk/government/publications/understanding-your-data-a-guide-for-school-governors-and-academy-trustees/understanding-your-data-a-guide-for-school-governors-and-academy-trustees

Working Together to Safeguard Children - www.gov.uk/government/publications/working-together-to-safeguard-children--2

Dictionary of edu acronyms

What on earth does that mean?

I'm going to be honest. When I started in my role as a school governor, I thought I had a pretty good handle on life in a school and the various nuances of education, but boy was I wrong. I got a rude awakening at my first governing body meeting when I realised every other item discussed related to an acronym I either didn't know or was unsure of, and I didn't want to look like an idiot by assuming wrongly. Of course, the right thing to do is put your hand up and say, 'Sorry, but what does XYZ mean?' but it's awkward if you feel like you might have to repeat that a dozen times during those first few meetings.

Of course, it's best practice to expand on any acronyms used in governing body meetings for the benefit of new members, but it never quite happens like that.

So how do we make those discussions, reports and minutes we need to read a bit more accessible? Well, over time I promise they all will be, but as a short cut I have pulled together as many of those pesky acronyms as I can remember into a handy governance dictionary (that might be an overstatement, but I'll go with it for now).

Hopefully this will be a useful guide to dip into when you aren't sure of a term or just a format to flick through when you have time to expand your edu-lingo!

I am sure I won't have remembered every possible term used, but hopefully it's a good foundation.

1:1 technology

One-to-one technology, often referred to as a 1:1 programme, simply provides one device for every student. The school will select the devices deemed most appropriate and install suitable administrative controls, and then the device will be assigned to the student for the duration of the academic year, or their time at school (perhaps a bit optimistic).

16-19 Bursary Fund

Funds to help with education-related costs for students aged 16-19 at a publicly funded school, on a training course or on unpaid work experience. Can be used to cover costs of required clothing/uniform, books, equipment, transport and food on the days of study.

Academic year

A nice easy one. The academic year runs from the autumn term (September) through to the end of the summer term the following year, ending in July. It's hopefully an obvious one, but important to remember that funding - depending on the status of your school - differs, with local authority schools working April to March for their financial year and academies working in line with the academic year of September to August for theirs.

Academies Financial Handbook

The Academies Financial Handbook has now been superseded by the Academy Trust Handbook.

Academy converter

Convertor status simply refers to schools that have chosen to become an academy through governing body resolution and application to the Secretary of State.

Academy sponsor

An academy sponsor is an organisation or person who has received approval from the Department for Education (DfE) to support an underperforming academy or group of academies. Sponsors work with the academies they support through their academy trust.

Any of the following can apply to become an academy sponsor:

- Schools
- Further education colleges
- Sixth form colleges
- Universities
- Businesses and entrepreneurs
- Educational foundations
- Charities and philanthropists
- Faith communities.

Academy sponsors are responsible for:

- Setting up the academy trust
- Appointing the leadership team
- Selecting the governing body
- Monitoring the academy's performance and acting where necessary
- Reporting to DfE about the academy's performance
- Involving parents and the wider community in the academy's work through events, mentoring and business links
- Making sure the academy spends its funding effectively
- Working with the academy trust, governing body, head, and senior leadership team.

If you don't comply with your responsibilities as sponsor, the Secretary of State for Education can remove your sponsor status.

Academy Trust Handbook

Also known as the Academies Financial Handbook, this is an important document all trustees should be familiar with. As the ESFA makes clear, 'academy trusts must comply with this handbook as a condition of their funding agreement. It provides an overarching framework for implementation of effective financial management and other controls, consistent with your obligations as publicly funded bodies' (ESFA, 2021).

You should read the Academy Trust Handbook if you have responsibility for governing, managing, or auditing an academy trust. This includes:

- Academy members, chairs of trusts, trustees, local governors and audit and risk committee members.
- Academy accounting officers, chief financial officers, and governance professionals (clerks to the board).
- Academy auditors.

The handbook comprises short topics explaining requirements that trusts must follow.

Accounting officer

Trustees must appoint an accounting officer; they should be an employee of your trust and they should be a senior executive leader. In single academy trusts this should be the headteacher/principal. In multi-academy trusts (MATs) it should be the CEO or executive head or equivalent. As you would expect, they must be a fit and suitable person for the role.

To use the official definition from the Academy Trust Handbook, 'the accounting officer role includes specific responsibilities for financial matters. It includes a personal responsibility to Parliament, and to the ESFA's accounting officer, for the trust's financial resources' (ESFA, 2021).

The accounting officer must have oversight of financial transactions, by:

- Ensuring the academy trust's property and assets are under the trustees' control, and measures exist to prevent losses or misuse.
- Ensuring bank accounts, financial systems and financial records are operated by more than one person.
- Keeping full and accurate accounting records to support their annual accounts.

It's very unlikely to happen, but your trust must get prior approval from the Education and Skills Funding Agency (ESFA) if, in exceptional circumstances, it wants to appoint an accounting officer who isn't a trust employee.

So, in almost all MATs, the CEO is the accounting officer. It doesn't mean they do the accounting, but part of their role is to have effective oversight of recording and reporting and have responsibility for the MAT's finances. It's a healthy reminder that most CEOs or executive heads come from a career as an educator and finance won't be their primary skill set. It's easy therefore to leave it to the trust's finance director or school business managers to manage the finances, but CEOs need to ensure they have sufficient visibility to check and challenge financial activities and reporting, as should the finance/audit committee on your board of trustees or local governing body.

If you are reading this as a trustee of a MAT, please also remember that the appointment of an accounting officer does not remove the trustees' responsibility for the proper conduct and financial operation of the trust.

As always, if in doubt it's worth checking the latest version of the Academy Trust Handbook - www.gov.uk/guidance/academy-trust-handbook/

Action tracker

An action tracker will be part of your document pack for each governing body meeting. It provides a summary of points raised 'for action' at previous meetings with any appropriate updates on progress or completion. Some governance professionals (clerks) tag the action on the end of the minutes for the previous meeting, and some issue a separate document. It's always a good idea to read this in advance and check there are no actions outstanding with your name next to them!

ADD - attention deficit disorder

This is now an out-of-date term for attention deficit hyperactivity disorder (ADHD).

ADHD - attention deficit hyperactivity disorder

ADHD is one of the most common neurodevelopmental disorders of childhood. It is usually first diagnosed in childhood and often lasts into adulthood. Children with ADHD may have trouble paying attention, controlling impulsive behaviours (may act without thinking about what the result will be), or be overly active.

Admissions policy

The admissions policy is important as fundamentally it defines (in priority order) which children will get places at your school.

Admissions criteria is different for each school and decided by the school (albeit in consultation with other stakeholders). As a handy starter, they may give priority to children:

- who live close to the school (see catchment area).
- who have a sibling already at the school.
- who have looked-after status (see LAC).
- who went to a particular primary school (a 'feeder school').
- who are eligible for the pupil premium or the service pupil premium.
- whose parent has worked at the school for two years or more.
- from a particular religion (for faith schools).
- who pass an entrance exam (for selective schools, i.e. grammar schools).

AEN – additional educational needs

AEN often refers to children with a wider set of needs or circumstances beyond SEND, for example, not being a native speaker (see EAL), traveller children, asylum seekers, etc.

AfL – Assessment for Learning

AfL is an acronym that is commonly used and stands for Assessment for Learning. At a very simplistic level it means that a teacher must be constantly assessing what the students in their classroom have learned, what they have yet to learn, and what their strengths and weaknesses are. That's the only simple bit; it is much more complex in delivery for individual students with such a diverse range of needs, abilities, strengths, and weaknesses.

AGM – annual general meeting

Yup, AGM simply denotes a meeting that you have on an annual basis.

AP – alternative provision

An alternative provision (AP) school, also sometimes called a pupil referral unit (see PRU). These schools provide education for children of compulsory school age who are unable to attend a mainstream or special school, sometimes because they are disengaged from education, at risk of being excluded or have been permanently excluded, and where additional nurture and support is needed.

At the time of writing, alongside my mainstream MAT chair role, I am also chair of an AP academy board.

APS – average point score

For key stage 2 and key stage 3 the APS is the average of the students' overall score in the tests for that age for maths, English and science. For key stage 4 (GCSEs), the APS is the average score for all the GCSE (or equivalent) exams the students take.

ARE – age-related expectations

Age-related expectations are based on what children should have learned, or should be able to do, at the end of each key stage. It works on the premise that the average child of that age and stage should meet a given standard.

Articles of association

As the NGA (www.nga.org.uk) explain, 'Academy trust articles of association stipulate the charitable purpose and the governance structure of the trust, including types of trustees and how they will be appointed or elected. They also set out other governance procedures including the arrangements for meetings and voting mechanisms' (National Governance Association, 2019).

Articles of association are a critical governance tool, helping you to comply with the law and providing key information about the purpose of the organisation, how it is to be run and to whom it is accountable. They should be regularly reviewed to ensure that they remain in line with the latest government expectations, are relevant and are able to provide you with the necessary powers to fulfil their purpose.

As a new (or existing) governor, it's important you have seen these. Some of the key information within your articles of association will be in the constitution of your trust – the constitution of your members and trustees – such as: majority of members cannot also be trustees, replacing members and trustees, what defines a quorum for meetings, having an AGM and more.

ASCL – Association of School and College Leaders

This is the Association of School and College Leaders and is the leading professional association and trade union for all school, college, and trust leaders. At the time of writing, they represented 21,500 school leaders in the UK. ASCL also provide a range of professional development courses, conferences, accreditations and more for school leaders.

Find out more at www.ascl.org.uk

ASD – autism spectrum disorder

'Autism, or Autism Spectrum Disorder (ASD), or Autism Spectrum Condition (ASC) - is a lifelong condition affecting how people communicate and interact with others and how they relate to the world about them.

'Autism is diagnosed by two elements: social communication difficulties and restricted, repetitive behaviours or interests. It can be described as a continuum of normal development or a spectrum, from mild, or high-functioning autism, often known as Asperger Syndrome, to a severe, non-verbal condition' (The Good Schools Guide, n. d.).

AST – advanced skills teacher

Sadly, the AST designation ceased in 2013. They were used to identify advanced teaching practitioners who were then assigned to share skills and support with other teachers in the school.

Asynchronous learning

A term that has become much more common since the arrival of the pandemic within the context of remote learning, asynchronous learning is simply where learning is done away from the real-time (see synchronous learning) teacher/ student lessons.

ATL - attitude to learning

Attitude to learning (ATL) is the way teachers assess and monitor students' approaches to their studies. Schools will adapt the key characteristics of good learning for their setting, but a good example is:

- Ready to learn - enthusiastic, attentive and organised.
- Resilient - positive, adaptable and confident.
- Resourceful - independent, focused and engaged.
- Respectful - polite, helpful and collaborative.
- Reflective - responsive, conscientious and considerate.

Attainment 8

Attainment 8 is a measure of academic performance in a secondary school. It is calculated by adding together a student's highest scores across eight government-approved school subjects. These numbers are not made publicly available on a pupil-by-pupil basis. Scores taken from across a school year group are averaged to produce a school's overall score.

The eight subjects are divided into three categories, often referred to as 'buckets':

Bucket 1
This contains English and maths, which are worth double marks, but the English will only count for double marks if both English literature and English language are taken. (Only the higher grade of the two is used.)

Bucket 2
The top three scores from the English Baccalaureate (see EBacc) subjects taken, i.e. sciences, computer science, history, geography, and languages (see MFL).

Bucket 3
Contains the top three scores from any remaining EBacc subjects or other approved qualifications i.e. other GCSEs or Level 2 certificates in some technical subjects.

The grades are then converted into points, put through a magic formula that is beyond me, and finally out comes the school's Attainment 8 score.

AUP – acceptable use policy

An acceptable use policy provides guidance and rules on the appropriate use of devices within the school. You would expect staff and students to sign this each year.

AWL – assessment without levels

The removal of assessing pupils against a 'level' allows schools to develop their own approaches to formative assessment – referred to as 'assessment without levels': the idea being that children could be assessed against what they knew from effective teaching, monitoring, feedback, and intervention.

> 'The removal of national curriculum levels in 2014 was designed to complement the introduction of a revised, more challenging national curriculum. The Commission on Assessment without Levels (CAWL) was set up to advise schools on the principles of effective assessment and to support and guide schools in developing their assessment policies and practice.
> 'In their report (CAWL, 2015) the commission argued that the removal of levels would provide an impetus for pedagogical change, increasing pupil motivation and engagement and making better use of formative assessment in the classroom. By removing levels with AWL, the intention was to reduce the time spent by teachers in recording and tracking progress towards numerical targets and release time for more in-depth teaching and formative assessment approaches that would support progress across the attainment spectrum.' (DfE, 2018)

AWPU – age-weighted pupil unit

AWPU is pretty key as this is where most of the funding for a school comes through, and the 'age-weighted' part is because the funding levels are different for primary- and secondary-age children.

Payment to the school is calculated based on the number of full-time children on roll at a school at the time of the January census, so for schools who are in a growth period, it can lead to a delay before funding is received for a child.

It's also worth being aware that this is not a common number for all schools across the country. The age-weighted pupil unit (AWPU) figure will be different in each local authority. Naturally, London schools have a higher level to reflect higher operational costs, but in some regions the discrepancies can be harder to explain.

BAME – black, Asian and minority ethnic

In March 2021, the Commission on Race and Ethnic Disparities recommended that the government stop using the term BAME. One of the recommendations in the final report on Covid-19 disparities, published in December 2021, was to refer to ethnic minority groups individually, rather than as a single group.

BAP – behaviour and attendance partnership

'Behaviour and attendance partnerships (BAP) enable schools to work together with other local services to address the needs of pupils with challenging behaviour.

'Some of the main priorities of a behaviour and attendance partnership are:

- improving overall levels of attendance and reducing persistent absence
- commissioning support for pupils with persistent absence
- devising joint attendance strategies
- identifying support for pupils who are at risk of exclusion
- ensuring that unofficial exclusions do not take place
- identifying placements for pupils with challenging behaviour where they have been excluded from schools or enter from another authority
- working with parent support advisors to develop school-home relationships
- promoting the consistent use of parenting contracts and parenting orders
- organising managed moves and effective early interventions
- putting in place systems for transition and re-integration between schools.' (Croner-i, 2015)

BEIS – Department for Business, Energy and Industrial Strategy

BEIS is the Department for Business, Energy and Industrial Strategy in the UK government.

Benchmarking

Benchmarking is defined as the process of measuring products, services, and processes against those of organisations known to be leaders in one or more aspects of their operations.

In a school setting, a benchmarking exercise could be comparing your costs for a provision, say school meals or the amount you spend on curriculum resources with other schools that have a similar context, so you can be reassured you are getting the best value for money. Often benchmarking against national averages will be used to reflect all aspects of your trust's performance, especially on academic performance, staff costs as a percentage of revenue and so on.

Whenever you are reviewing your school accounts and reflecting on major financial commitments for service provision, it's important to ask if your school has ever undertaken any benchmarking, similarly for workforce costs, just to ensure you have provided suitable challenge and are satisfied your school is operating (where appropriate) within the normal range.

BESA - British Education Suppliers Association

Many of the vendors your school engages with for your classroom and curriculum software will be members of BESA. BESA is the trade association for the UK education supplier's sector. They operate on a not-for-profit basis and are accountable to an executive council elected by member companies. They are also part of the delivery team for the Bett show each year in London and actively support UK vendors supplying their solutions internationally. They are a great resource that we are lucky to have.

Bett

Bett are at the centre of the global community for education technology. In your role as a governor or trustee of a school or MAT, you may well have an opportunity to visit the Bett show at the London ExCel each January (note: moved to March for 2023 before returning to its usual date, the last week of January). They also organise similar, albeit smaller events internationally in Asia and Brazil.

The Bett show is a great fusion of the latest educational technology (see EdTech) solutions alongside loads of great training sessions and panel discussions. I would recommend it for any governor who wants to get a broader sense of some of the digital solutions now available for schools and to be able to be part of your school's discussions around its digital vision.

To find out more, visit: www.bettshow.com

BFR - budget forecast return

The BFR is a return made annually by multi-academy trusts to the ESFA sharing their three-year budget plans and associated cash flow forecasts. It's how the ESFA can identify trusts that have trending financial risks.

BIS - Department for Business, Innovation and Skills

The BIS is a UK government department that merged recently with the Department for Energy and Climate Change and formed the new Department for Business, Energy and Industrial Strategy (See BEIS).

Blended learning

Blended learning is a method of teaching that combines online and face-to-face activities. Students usually have some control over time, place, and pace. (Post-Covid-19, it can also refer to a mixture of asynchronous and synchronous learning.)

BME - black and minority ethnic

In March 2021, the Commission on Race and Ethnic Disparities recommended that the government stop using the term BME. One of the recommendations in the final report on Covid-19 disparities, published in December 2021, was to refer to ethnic minority groups individually, rather than as a single group.

BoG - board of governors

Another way of saying local governing body. A term more typically used within schools in Northern Ireland.

Breach of data

It has always been the case (but never more so than post GDPR introduction) that your school will need to have robust procedures to deal with data protection breaches. A data breach is anything leading to the accidental or unlawful destruction, loss, alteration or unauthorised disclosure of, or access to, personal data.

Most breaches are the result of human error, such as sending one child's report card to another child's parent, leaving your laptop unlocked in a classroom and leaving it unsupervised, sharing a login with another member of staff, sending the wrong data filled document to the wrong recipients, the list goes on. Any of these constitute a data breach and need to be reported to your data protection officer (DPO) and logged in your school or trust's central data breach log, alongside details of the steps the school took to mitigate and avoid breaches in future. Where the breach is significant it needs to be reported to the Information Commissioner's Office (ICO) as well.

To find out more, visit www.ico.org.uk

BTEC

A BTEC or 'Business and Technology Education Council' (the name of the body which originally oversaw it) is a practical-based, vocational qualification. It can be studied at a college or school.

BTECs provide the opportunity to gain hands-on experience in a field or subject and are a viable alternative to the more theory-focused, classroom-based ways of learning that some students might be put off by. BTECs are a popular path to both university and particular jobs in place of, or in addition to, A-levels. While they are commonly known as an alternative to A-levels, BTEC qualifications can be studied at a number of levels, including GCSE and even degree level.

Originally, funding for most BTECs was due to be phased out between 2023 and 2025. There is a government focus to transition to the use of the new technical T-Levels alongside traditional A-Levels. In November 2021 Michelle Donelan MP, however, indicated that this was not the plan and that they were not abolishing BTECs, so there is likely to be just a narrowing field of course options in the coming years.

BYOD - bring your own device

BYOD relates to schools' digital strategies where children can use their own personal technology within the classroom. Most commonly this will be a programme where parents are encouraged to provide their child with a laptop that can be brought to school or the use of tablets and phones in some settings. It can be helpful where budget limits school IT, but there are lots of practical considerations in terms of security, IT policy and data protection to consider, as well as the broader management of the device.

It was a very popular topic for discussion a few years ago, but many projects proved too complicated to manage. Schools have found initiatives where each child is assigned a device (from the school) to be more effective and easier to maintain (see 1:1 technology).

CAF - Common Assessment Framework

The Common Assessment Framework was used by social workers to gather information about a child or young person. The CAF is used when local authority social care teams have concerns that the needs of a child or young person are not being met.

The CAF provided a set format and structure for assessing a child's needs throughout England and Wales. The purpose of it is to try to deliver consistency in assessment and decision making.

All children and young people identified as having special educational needs or additional learning needs were likely to require an assessment through the Common Assessment Framework. That was to establish whether there were any services or support that social care could provide.

In recent years, the Common Assessment Framework has been replaced by the Early Help Assessment (EHA). The EHA is based on the same principles as the CAF, but it is much simpler and more straightforward to use.

CAMHS - Child and Adolescent Mental Health Services

CAMHS is a service that works with children and young people who have emotional and/or behavioural difficulties. CAMHS services generally support young people experiencing:

- sadness, low mood, or depression
- feelings of worry or anxiety
- low confidence
- problems with eating or their relationship with food
- anger
- problems sleeping
- hearing voices or seeing things
- thoughts about wanting to hurt themselves
- difficult feelings after a traumatic event.

Each CAMHS centre is a multi-disciplinary team, normally consisting of:

- psychiatrists and psychologists
- social workers
- nurses
- support workers
- occupational therapists
- specialist substance misuse workers.

CARS - childhood autism rating scale

Childhood autism rating scale is used to assess for autistic traits. Now on its second version (CARS2) it is designed as a clinical rating scale for the trained clinician to rate items indicative of autism spectrum disorder (ASD) after direct observation of the child. The form is used with individuals of all ages and in both clinical and research settings.

Cashless

In a school context, cashless is where schools no longer require students to carry cash to pay for their meals and other associated costs. Most commonly nowadays, students are registered with their fingerprint on a biometric system that allows all meals and additional purchases to be automatically charged to their account.

CAT - cognitive ability test

A cognitive abilities test (CAT) is used by UK schools to assess pupils' developed abilities and future academic potential.

Schools use a child's performance in a CAT to judge progress over the academic year and to make decisions regarding setting and streaming according to ability. It is a way for a school to understand a pupil's strengths and weaknesses and to personalise learning and adapt teaching. It is also used by some schools as part of their entry process into Year 7 (11+).

Catchment area

Just think of a nice, neat ring around your school covering your local community. OK, your catchment area won't be as simple or neat as that, but a catchment is a defined geographical area surrounding a school from which it will usually take most of its pupils. Expect your catchment area to be a key part of your admissions policy.

CCEA

For our educators from Northern Ireland, the CCEA is the Council for the Curriculum, Examinations and Assessment. Find out more at https://ccea.org.uk

Clinical commissioning group

One you will hopefully come across infrequently in school discussions, but your local CCG is made up of groups of professionals that are responsible for commissioning health services within your region.

CCMS - Council for Catholic Maintained Schools

The term CCMS is often used alongside their DECs - Diocesan Education Committees - which oversee Catholic maintained schools in Northern Ireland.

CD&I - culture, diversity and inclusion

In a nutshell, CD&I is about empowering people by respecting and appreciating what makes them different, in terms of age, gender, ethnicity, religion, disability, sexual orientation, education and national origin.

CDT - craft, design and technology

CEIAG - careers education, information, advice and guidance

A careers education, information, advice and guidance (CEIAG) strategy and implementation plan is designed to prepare students for life in modern Britain by providing the knowledge, understanding, confidence and skills that they need to make informed choices and plans for their future learning and career.

CELF - Clinical Evaluation of Language Fundamentals

The Clinical Evaluation of Language Fundamentals (CELF) is a comprehensive assessment that can be used to assess all aspects of a child's communication, including receptive language, expressive language, phonological awareness (speech sounds), and pragmatic skills.

CEOP - Child Exploitation and Online Protection

CEOP is a law enforcement agency that aims to keep children and young people safe from sexual exploitation and abuse. Online sexual abuse can be reported on their website and a report made to one of its child protection advisors.

CFC - cared-for children

Also known as looked-after children (see LAC).

CfE - Curriculum for Excellence

The Curriculum for Excellence (CfE) is the Scottish alternative to the English national curriculum. There are three core subjects that schools must ensure are taught: health and wellbeing, literacy, and numeracy.

CFR - Consistent Financial Reporting

The Consistent Financial Reporting (CFR) Framework provides a template for schools to collect information about their income and expenditure by financial years. The CFR framework applies to maintained schools and pupil referral units. It's optional for nurseries and non-maintained special schools.

CIF - Condition Improvement Fund

You may well come across CIF bids where your school is looking to make improvements to your school infrastructure and is seeking financial support from the ESFA. CIF bids are often time limited with an expectation that, once approved, the funding will be committed or spent by the following March.

CIN - Children in Need Plan

A Children in Need (CIN) Plan is drawn up following a single assessment, which identifies the child as having complex needs and where a coordinated response is needed in order for the child's needs to be met.

Clerk to the governing body

Replaced in 2021 to be called a 'governance professional', but I think we all still think of and refer to the term clerk to the governing body. (See governance professional for more information.)

Cloud (the)

Nothing mysterious here, the Cloud is just a term to describe a group of servers and applications hosted remotely on someone else's infrastructure, which is accessible from anywhere. This could be Microsoft or Amazon, but it could be your school creating a 'private' cloud for restricted access.

CME - Children Missing Education

Children Missing Education (CME) refers to all children who are of compulsory school age (September following their 5th birthday), who are not on a school roll, or being educated otherwise (e.g. privately or in alternative provision) and who have been out of any educational provision for a substantial period of time.

Coasting schools

No, not linked to the proximity of the sea - coasting schools are those deemed to be doing OK, but are not showing any indicators of continued improvement.

At primary, the DfE benchmark at the time of writing is in schools where over a two-year period less than 85% of children receive a level 4 in reading, writing and maths and that have below average proportions of children making expected progress between ages 7 and 11.

At secondary schools, the simplistic measure of 'coasting' is schools with an attainment level at below 60% over a two-year period and where their Progress 8 measure is consistently below -0.25. In truth it's a bit more complicated than that, but for the purpose of this book it hopefully provides the basics for a coasting school and shows that it is not something you would want to be identified as.

Co-ed

Co-ed or co-educational simply refers to a school where all genders attend. It tends to only be in the independent sector (and some grammar schools) where schools choose to have cohorts of only boys or girls.

CofG - chair of governors

Sometimes elected by the governing body, in MATs often elected by trustees, the chair of governors is a key role in the leadership and management of schools. Think of the role in the context of first amongst equals.

To be effective, they need a good understanding of their role and responsibilities so that the school gains maximum benefit from the work that the governing body does.

The key role of the chair includes:

- **Leading effective governance**: giving the governing body a clear lead and direction, ensuring that the governors work as an effective team and understand their accountability and the part they play in the strategic leadership of the school and in driving school improvement.
- **Building the team**: attracting governors with the necessary skills and ensuring that tasks are delegated across the governing body so that all members contribute, and feel that their individual skills, knowledge, and experience are well used and that the overall workload is shared.
- **Relationship with the headteacher**: being a critical friend by offering support, challenge and encouragement, holding the headteacher to

account and ensuring the headteacher's performance management is rigorous and robust; a good comparison is with the role of the chair of a board of trustees who works with the chief executive of an organisation but does not run day-to-day operations.

- **Improving your school**: ensuring school improvement is the focus of all policy and strategy and that governor scrutiny, monitoring and challenge reflect school improvement priorities.

- **Leading the business**: ensuring that statutory requirements and regulations are met, that the school provides value for money in its use of resources and that governing body business is conducted efficiently and effectively. (National College for Teaching & Leadership, 2014)

CP – child protection

Child protection is part of the safeguarding process. It focuses on protecting individual children identified as suffering or likely to suffer significant harm (abuse, neglect, health and wellbeing).

CPD – continuous personal development

CPD can refer to continuous personal development or sometimes continuous professional development or even just PD, albeit we don't really want to lose the continuous bit. It is simply the term used to describe the learning activities professionals engage in to develop and enhance their abilities. As a governor or trustee reading this book, you have already embarked on your own CPD journey, so well done!

CQ – cultural intelligence

Cultural intelligence (CQ) is a globally recognised way of assessing and improving effectiveness in culturally diverse situations. It's the ability to relate and work effectively with people from different cultural backgrounds and it goes beyond existing notions of cultural sensitivity and awareness.

If you want to know why there is a Q in that acronym, it's because it is also known as a cultural quotient, which is derived from IQ.

CST - Confederation of School Trusts

The Confederation of School Trusts (CST) is the national organisation and sector body for school trusts in England advocating for, connecting, and supporting executive and governance leaders.

To find out more see: www.cstuk.org.uk

CVA - contextual value added

Contextual value added (CVA) is a measure used as a performance indicator that considers factors from outside the classroom, including gender, special educational needs and disabilities (SEND), movement between schools, looked-after children (LAC) and family circumstances that are all likely to impact on a student's performance.

D&T (or DT)

Short for the design & technology department or course.

DBS - Disclosure and Barring Service

As a governor or trustee, you will likely encounter this term under the umbrella of a 'DBS check'. The intention of the DBS is to help all employers make safer recruitment decisions, and as you would expect, all staff within a school undertake one (including externally contracted staff for any student-facing activities). As governors who will have access to and potentially be left unsupervised in a school setting, it is also a requirement that we all have a DBS check. In fact, currently we must all undertake an 'Enhanced' DBS check.

There are currently four levels of DBS checks available from the Disclosure and Barring Service. These are a basic DBS check, a standard DBS check, an enhanced DBS check and an enhanced with barred lists DBS check.

Within the context of schools and the enhanced DBS check, this certificate will contain details of both spent and unspent convictions, cautions, reprimands, and warnings that are held on the Police National Computer, which are not subject to filtering. The certificate may also contain non-conviction information supplied by relevant police forces if it is deemed relevant and ought to be contained in the certificate. In addition, the check can contain a check against one of the DBS barred lists.

It's a simple process to undertake requiring you to share some key personal details (address, passport or driving licence, photo ID, etc.) and depending on the system, typically it only takes a few weeks to process. You will also want to check for a similar certificate if you are sitting on a panel undertaking staff recruitment as part of your safer recruitment obligations.

You can find out more here: www.gov.uk/government/organisations/disclosure-and-barring-service

Declaration of interest

You would make a declaration of interest if a subject or topic on your agenda covered something where you may have any direct or indirect conflict in relation to it. So, if your governing body are discussing who to contract for their school meals and you are head chef at 'Meals4Schools', then you would make that clear at the start of the meeting, and step outside while that topic is discussed.

(See also pecuniary interest.)

DEI – diversity, equity and inclusion

Diversity, equity and inclusion (DEI) is a term used to describe policies and programmes that promote the representation and participation of different groups of individuals, including people of different ages, races and ethnicities, disabilities, genders, religions, cultures, and sexual orientations. This also covers people with diverse backgrounds, experiences, skills, and expertise.

DENI – Department of Education in Northern Ireland

Find out more at www.education-ni.gov.uk

Design thinking

The design thinking process involves five steps: empathise, define, ideate (form an idea), prototype, and test. Used in classrooms, students can learn to solve problems, invent, and create solutions by using the same process.

As shared by the Interaction Design Foundation, design thinking is an iterative process in which you seek to understand your users, challenge assumptions, redefine problems and create innovative solutions which you can prototype and test. The overall goal is to identify alternative strategies and solutions that are not instantly apparent with your initial level of understanding.

Design thinking is more than just a process; it opens an entirely new way to think, and it offers a collection of hands-on methods to help you apply this new mindset. In essence, design thinking:

- Revolves around a deep interest to understand the people for whom we design products and services.
- Helps us observe and develop empathy with the target users.
- Enhances our ability to question. In design thinking you question the problem, the assumptions, and the implications.
- Proves extremely useful when you tackle problems that are ill-defined or unknown.
- Involves ongoing experimentation through sketches, prototypes, testing and trials of new concepts and ideas.

Find out more at: www.interaction-design.org

DFC – devolved formula capital (grant)

Your school's devolved formula capital (DFC) grant is the capital funding allocated for each school by the DfE funding formula. At its simplest level, it provides schools capital funding to allow them to prioritise the maintenance of their buildings and grounds, alongside providing funding for investment in equipment including ICT.

Sadly, it is far from sufficient in most cases, with typical funding in 2022 for a primary school at just over £11 per pupil and closer to £17 for a secondary school. The amount is almost double for a specialist or PRU setting.

DHoS – deputy head of school
DHT – deputy headteacher

DI – diversity and inclusion

Diversity is about representation or the make-up of your school cohort and staff. Inclusion is about how well the contributions, presence, and perspectives of those different groups of people are valued and integrated into the school environment and ethos.

DigCit – digital citizenship

Digital citizenship (DigCit) is the ability to access digital technologies safely and responsibly, as well as being an active and respectful member of society, both online and offline. It's a broad topic and within your school it will cover many strands including, not least, equity of access to technology, students' digital skills, how to appropriately communicate online, keeping data safe/cyber security, freedom of speech and digital wellbeing, as well as the skills to research and challenge the validity of information.

Digital strategy

Every school identifies that it has a need for technology, and when technology is used in the right way, it can have a positive impact. But at the same time, with financial budgets and pressures on schools, it's difficult to know – and choose – where those precious funds are best spent.

My advice and belief is always that the best starting point is to have a digital strategy; a plan of what you want to achieve and why. First and foremost, it should be driven by educators and leaders in terms of outcomes, and secondly, it should tally with the financial and budgetary opportunities of the school.

In lots of schools, and particularly in groups of schools, the driver for implementing new technology is often determined by the finance function saying, 'We have this much to spend – what would you like?' Although that has a degree of sense, it's the wrong way round to start a digital strategy. The impetus should perhaps instead come from the educators in the classroom, setting out the things they want to do and deciding on the tools that they believe will have a positive impact on learning.

You can find out loads more in my book *My Secret #EdTech Diary* published by John Catt, which shapes the process of creating your school's digital strategy, as well as providing governors with the right questions to ask.

DPIA – data protection impact assessment

A data protection impact assessment (DPIA) describes a process designed to identify risks arising out of the processing of personal data and to minimise these risks as far and as early as possible. DPIAs are important tools for negating risk and for demonstrating compliance with the GDPR.

For the avoidance of doubt, a data protection impact assessment must always be conducted when the processing of staff or students' data could result in a high risk to their rights and freedoms. In essence, that's any solutions you use to capture and store student data, curriculum apps with individual student accounts, your school CCTV system and so on.

DPO – data protection officer

The DPO role involves advising school leadership and staff about their data obligations and monitoring compliance, including managing internal data protection activities, training, and conducting internal audits.

The DPO will also need to advise on when data protection impact assessments (see DPIA) are required and be available for data protection enquiries from parents and pupils. Additionally, they need to be able to report directly to the board and be the point of contact for communication with the Information Commissioner.

The data protection officer needs to be:

- Highly knowledgeable about data protection, GDPR, the school's operations, technology, and security.
- Well placed to promote a data protection culture within a school.

This is a really important role that you must have established in every school or trust and that everyone knows how to contact. This could be someone internally or an external person or provider facilitating the role.

You will have a data protection/privacy policy at your school already and as a new governor you should check to see who your school's DPO is, as anyone who discovers a breach of data will need to be able to report it directly to them.

I'd also strongly recommend you take a bit of time and check out the DfE's '**Data protection: toolkit for schools**', which can be found here: www.gov.uk/government/publications/data-protection-toolkit-for-schools

DSAR – data subject access request

A data subject access request (DSAR) is a submission by an individual (data subject) asking to know what personal information of theirs has been collected and stored by the school and how it is being used.

DSG – dedicated schools grant

The dedicated schools grant (DSG) is a ring-fenced block of money that goes to each local authority for distribution to schools as their basic funding. Funding is based on an amount per child for each school. The amount varies based on several factors, and in calculating the share of the grant for each school, the local authority will retain a slice of the funding towards the costs of your LA's 'children's services' provision and, based on local board agreement, potentially retain some for additional support towards their 'high needs' funding.

DSL – designated safeguarding lead

The designated safeguarding lead (formerly known as the child protection officer) is 'the person appointed to make sure that schools and colleges adhere to their safeguarding policies' (Inside Government, 2020).

While every member of staff in your school should be up to date with their safeguarding training and should understand the safeguarding policies and procedures for the school, the DSLs take an extra responsibility for safeguarding.

Ultimately, the role of the designated safeguarding lead is to act as the first point of contact for any safeguarding or child protection incident or concern in the setting and even sometimes outside of the workplace.

According to Keeping Children Safe in Education 2022 (KCSIE), every school and college should have a designated safeguarding lead who will provide support to staff to carry out their safeguarding duties and who will liaise closely with other services such as children's social care.

Dyscalculia

Children with dyscalculia have difficulty in acquiring mathematical skills.

Dyslexia

Children with dyslexia have a marked and persistent difficulty in learning to read, write and spell, despite progress in other areas.

Dyspraxia

Pupils with dyspraxia are affected by an impairment or immaturity of the organisation of movement, often appearing clumsy.

EAL – English as an additional language

EAL is one of several acronyms used to describe the teaching of English where it is not a person's first language. This is the acronym most used in UK schools, but some may use a different version such as ESL (English as a second language).

Early Years

For Early Years see 'EYFS', which covers nursery- and reception-aged children between 3 and 5.

EBacc – English Baccalaureate

Keeping it nice and simple, the English Baccalaureate (EBacc) is a performance measure for any student who achieves good GCSE or accredited certificate passes in English, mathematics, history/geography, two sciences and a language.

This is a topic I would expect you to discuss as part of your school curriculum or standards meetings. There is a national expectation for schools to aim for 90% of their students to be entered for the EBacc by 2025. In 2020-21 only 38% of children nationally were entered for the EBacc, which was slightly down on prior years. For many schools the requirement of a language subject particularly (see MFL) presents a barrier to entry for a proportion of their cohort.

It will likely be a discussion your school will have between meeting national expectations versus ensuring we enter our students for subjects they have the best chance of success with. I would argue that, under the umbrella of inclusivity for all students, the EBacc has challenges, and I would encourage schools and governing bodies to be confident in defending their position on submissions each year.

See www.schoolsweek.co.uk/ebacc-target-even-further-off-as-entries-fall-again/

EBD – emotional and behavioural difficulties

ECM – Every Child Matters
A legacy term now, Every Child Matters (ECM) was replaced with the term 'help children achieve more' (Puffett, 2010).

ECM was built around five key strands, namely every child shall be: staying safe, being healthy, enjoying and achieving, achieving economic wellbeing, and making a positive contribution to society. Each of these aims were subject to a detailed framework whereby multi-agency partnerships work together to achieve the objectives of the initiative.

ECT – early career teacher
Replacing the previous newly qualified teacher (NQT) status, as of March 2021 early career teachers (ECTs) now undertake a two-year period of induction once they start their first teaching role.

In addition to the 10% timetable reduction that ECTs receive in their first year of induction, ECTs will also receive a 5% timetable reduction in the second year of induction. The role of an ECT mentor has been introduced. The mentor will have a key role in supporting the ECT during their induction.

EDI – equality, diversity and inclusion
(See DEI.)

EdTech - educational technology

The most common definition is a short and snappy 'educational technology is the combined use of computer hardware, software and educational theory and practice to facilitate learning'. That said, with the ever growing role of technology within our schools, I explain in my book (*My Secret #EdTech Diary*, John Catt Publishers, 2021) that this is now too narrow a lens to view it through.

When we talk about EdTech, our natural inclination is to consider it solely within the context of the learning environment - i.e. the classroom (or more recently, the online classroom) - but actually, I believe educational technology should be considered in a much wider context as it represents the effective use of technology in any part of the educational setting - whether it's to support your school, your trust, or your district.

It's fair to acknowledge that 90% of the narrative around educational technology relates to supporting effective teaching and learning; however, we also know that the right technology, when deployed more widely, can improve operational efficiency and communication which, in turn, can free up valuable time and (with the right tools) precious money to go back into our classrooms. So, when we think about the wider deployment of digital technology within our schools, the more we can save and the more efficient we can become in the broader operation of our schools, the more flexibility and funds we have available to focus on our core priority - teaching and learning.

So, while the original definition isn't wrong, perhaps we can redefine educational technology, especially when planning for the future, as 'any computer hardware, software, device or service intended for deployment within an educational setting'. After all, it would be easy to exclude a Wi-Fi access point from the original definition, yet it's pretty key to the use of, for example, tablets in the library. You may agree with me that it's a rather broad definition (and it is) but in reality, the role technology plays within the operation of any school is huge and covers so many strands, it's counter-intuitive to try to define it as one single thing.

EHA - Early Help Assessment

The Common or Early Help Assessment process replaces the previous CAF assessment and is also referred to as Family Assessment.

A Common or Early Help Assessment process is a way of gathering information about children and the whole family in one place and using it to help decide what type of support is needed to help a family. People from different organisations will talk to one another, share information with parents' consent and work together with them to help to provide support.

EHCP - education and health care plan

An EHCP describes the special educational needs that a child or young person has and the help that will be given to meet them. It also includes the health and care provision that is needed. It is a legal document written by the local authority and is used for children and young people who have high support needs.

You will likely encounter these in many of your discussions as a governor, normally within the context for your SEND meetings. Often the biggest challenge is the process required to secure an EHCP for a child. Provision of an EHCP for a child also includes additional funding for the school to contribute towards any additional support they might require.

Schools are provided with additional money to provide support for children with SEND; this is called their delegated budget. Each child with SEND is entitled to receive up to £6000 of funding from their school per year. Beyond this, funding is provided by the local authority based on the details of support needed in their plan.

EHE - electively home educated

An EHE is a term used to describe a choice by parents to provide education for their children at home or in some other way they desire, instead of sending them to school full-time.

EIF - Education Inspection Framework

The Education Inspection Framework (EIF) sets out how Ofsted inspects maintained schools, academies, non-association independent schools, further education and skills provision and registered Early Years settings in England.

ELG – early learning goal

Early learning goals (ELG) are the goals or targets for children to achieve at the end of their reception year. They will be working towards these goals throughout the EYFS.

EMA – Education Maintenance Allowance

An Education Maintenance Allowance is a financial incentive paid to post-16 students to keep them in full-time education. At the time of writing, this is no longer available in England but is still available in Scotland, Wales, and Northern Ireland.

In England, a student would apply for funding from the 16-19 Bursary fund.

EOE – equal opportunity employer

An equal opportunity employer simply means an employer who is committed to a policy of treating all its employees and job applicants equally.

EP – educational psychologist

An educational psychologist (EP) supports schools and families where the child or young person is having difficulties in school with learning, behaviour, or emotions. It is worth noting that for many schools there is a real challenge in terms of availability of educational psychologists, and this can really slow the process of getting suitable support packages in place for your children.

EPQ – Extended Project Qualification

Extended Project Qualifications are a sixth-form qualification that involve students choosing a topic, carrying out research, creating a report (or 'product' and report) and delivering a presentation.

The 'Good Schools Guide' explains better than I could what's involved:

'There are several types of EPQ - students can write a research-based report, put on an event like a charity fundraiser, make something such as a piece of art or model or put on a performance such as a musical. Other options include producing a piece of creative writing or multimedia. But although the choices are wide and varied, students must show that it is academically useful, either relating to their current course of study or future career.

'A research-based project involves writing a dissertation (usually 5,000 words); alternatives are backed up with a 1,000-word report. The final stage is a 10-15 minute presentation to a group of non-specialists about your topic. Students are expected to spend around 120 hours on their EPQ - although some take more time, others less. Students can expect support and guidance from a supervisor (normally a teacher) and most do their research in the summer holidays following year 12 and complete the project in the first term of year 13.

'EPQs are currently graded A* to E and they are worth up to half an A level, as well as UCAS points. An A* in the EPQ is worth 70 UCAS points, an A 60, B 50, C 40, D 30 and an E 20. (The Good Schools Guide, n. d.)

Find out more at www.goodschoolsguide.co.uk

ESFA

This stands for the Education and Skills Funding Agency. The ESFA are sponsored by the Department for Education and are the body accountable for funding education and skills for children, young people, and adults. In essence, this is where the money comes from to fund all our core school activities.

ESL - English as a second language

(Also see EAL.) ESL is one of several acronyms used to describe the teaching of English where it is not a person's first language.

ESOL - English for speakers of other languages

ESOL is sometimes offered for parents and community support.

Estyn - education and training inspectorate for Wales

Think of them as the Welsh equivalent of Ofsted... or Ofsted as the English equivalent of Estyn!

Ever 6 FSM

This is when a student has a historic free school meals (FSM) status. They will be classed as Ever 6 FSM for 6 years after their FSM eligibility end date.

EWO – education welfare officer

Predominantly the role of an education welfare officer (EWO) is to work closely with the school and parents to ensure all children are attending school or receiving approximate education. They will typically meet parents and students at school (or home) to explain their legal responsibilities, help families get benefits for school meals, transport, clothing, and so on.

Executive headteacher

Typically an experienced head who has responsibilities for schools within a MAT. The term is nowadays often interchangeable with a trust CEO, depending on the desire to have a more education- or corporate-focused title. In my MAT, for example, we have an executive headteacher rather than a CEO title.

Extended schools

Extended schools often refer to schools that provide a range of activities and support beyond the normal school day that may be of benefit to not just students but also families and the broader community. Many trusts and schools already offer extended provision, but this is a more formalised description.

EYFS

EYFS is the Early Years Foundation Stage, often referred to in the daily context as your reception classes. It covers both nursery and reception for ages 3 to 5.

Fair banding

A pretty rare one now, but this is part of an admissions process whereby a school splits potential students into bands based on ability. The school then admits the same number of students from each band.

FAP - Fair Access Protocol

The Fair Access Protocol (FAP) is 'a mechanism developed by the local authority in partnership with all schools in their area. Its aim is to ensure that vulnerable children, and those who are having difficulty in securing a school place in-year, are allocated a school place as quickly as possible' (DfE, 2021).

FERPA

Relevant to our US readers, this is the Family Educational Rights and Privacy Act (FERPA). It's a federal law that is designed to protect the privacy of students' educational records.

FFT - Fischer Family Trust

Fischer Family Trust (FFT) is an independent charity that provides educational data and resources for schools.

'Our online system, FFT Aspire, is used by over 13,600 schools LAs, MATs and chains in England and Wales (as of Aug 2022). Their estimates are used by teachers to inform the setting of ambitious and aspirational targets for students. They analyse pupil results and pupil progress and provide school leaders with insightful data to support school improvement and self-evaluation' (FFT, n. d.).

You can find out more here - www.fft.org.uk

FGM - female genital mutilation

Female genital mutilation (FGM) is a procedure where the female genitals are deliberately cut, injured, or changed, but there's no medical reason for this to be done. It's also known as female circumcision or cutting. Schools will ensure that information about this is shared in private spaces so that students can safely report their concerns.

Flipped classroom

Increasingly referenced, in essence a flipped classroom is where the students first gain exposure of a new topic and resources outside of the classroom, learn the basics and then use subsequent classroom time to build on that knowledge and embed it. Think of it as the opposite of a lesson followed by homework.

FLO - family liaison officer

A family liaison officer (FLO) in the United Kingdom is a police officer, either uniformed or part of the Criminal Investigation Department, trained to act as a liaison between the police and families who have been victims of crime.

FOI - freedom of information

Within the context of your students' data held by the school, you may encounter a freedom of information request from a parent seeking copies of all data on their child. This is not the only scenario, but the most common a school might encounter.

Formative assessment

This is where evaluating a student's learning is done during their topic/unit. There are all sorts of tools available for undertaking formative assessment - quick quizzing tools and surveys, for example. (See summative assessment for alternative.)

Free schools

Free schools, much like academies, are all-ability state schools that have been built in response to specific local demand, most notably lack of choice for parents, and are not run by a local authority. They can be established by an organisation or group of individuals subject to a successful application in each wave of DfE funding rounds.

FSM - free school meals

In addition to universal infant free school meals (see UIFSM), older children can also qualify for free school meals (FSM) at school if their parents receive any of the following:

- Income Support
- Income-based Jobseeker's Allowance
- Income-related Employment and Support Allowance
- Support under Part VI of the Immigration and Asylum Act 1999
- The guaranteed element of Pension Credit

- Child Tax Credit (provided they are not also entitled to Working Tax Credit)
- Working Tax Credit run-on
- Universal Credit (up to a limit).

If a child is eligible for free school meals, they'll remain eligible until they finish the phase of schooling (primary or secondary).

There are slightly different processes for applying in England, Wales, Scotland and Northern Ireland.

FTE – fixed term exclusion

A fixed term exclusion is excluding a child from school for a specific period. A pupil may be excluded for one or more fixed periods (up to a maximum of 45 school days in a single academic year). The law does not allow for extending a fixed term exclusion or 'converting' a fixed term exclusion into a permanent exclusion (see PermEx).

FTE – full-time equivalent

You are likely to encounter this on your personnel committee when reviewing staff numbers. The FTE is the headcount of full-time staff plus the proportion of the full-time hours worked by part-time teachers.

FTS – Find a Tender service

From 1 January 2021, a new procurement process came into play. Since the UK left the EU, a new system was needed to replace that of OJEU (Official Journal of the European Union). So, the government introduced the Find a Tender service, or FTS for short.

GAG – general annual grant

Stands for general annual grant. It is an academy's main bulk of funding each year and represents each of their schools' share of the dedicated schools grant (see DSG), which is paid to each local authority for distribution to schools.

Gamification

Gamification is an approach for engaging students more deeply in learning through game design principles and mechanics. Often this can be by building in competitions, daily scores, or simply learning concepts through perceived play.

GCSE

Hopefully this one isn't a surprise term. GCSE stands for General Certificate of Secondary Education - the examinations taken by students in England.

GDPR

The General Data Protection Regulation is a regulation in EU law on data protection and privacy in the European Union and the European Economic Area. Within a school setting it's all about keeping any personal data safe and secure, controlling who has access to it and how long you keep it for.

GIAS - Get Information about Schools

GIAS is the Department for Education's (DfE) register of educational establishments in England and Wales. It contains vital information about children's centres, academies, free schools, maintained schools, independent schools, further education colleges (further education and sixth form corporations, specialist designated colleges and special post-16 institutions) and higher education institutions.

You can find out more at www.get-information-schools.service.gov.uk

GNVQ - General National Vocational Qualifications

A GNVQ was similar to a BTEC and the advanced GNVQ was equivalent of 2 A-levels. The subjects offered had a vocational element.

Governance professional

A nice new name for what was our clerk to the governing body. The National Governance Association (NGA) summarises the role as: 'Governance professionals are paid to provide administrative and advisory support to governing boards. They make an invaluable contribution to board efficiency, effectiveness, productivity and compliance. They also have a crucial role in promoting the culture that ensures good governance in schools and trusts.'

'The governance professional is the 'constitutional conscience' of the governing board. They provide advice on governance, constitutional and procedural matters. They also offer administrative support to the governing board and relay information on legal requirement' (National Governance Association, 2021b).

On a personal level, it's safe to say I think they are key, and as a chair of a trust board, having a good working relationship with a great governance professional (clerk) is essential. Mine makes me look way better organised and informed than I really am! Thank you, Emily.

Governing body

I'm hoping you know this one already if you are reading this book, but for the avoidance of doubt, here is a nice, neat definition: a governing body is a group of people responsible for the strategic running of a school. They are usually comprised of the headteacher, staff governors, parent governors, community governors and governors appointed by the local authority (unless the school is part of an academy).

Sadly it's not quite as simple as that, as within academies, the local governing body isn't responsible for the strategic aspects of school delivery. In fact, in most cases finance, HR and strategic planning will be handled by the trust board, so the local governing body (LGB) focuses on the curriculum delivery, health and safety, and broader successful operation of the school, supporting and challenging the school leadership. I cover governing bodies in more detail earlier in this book.

As a handy reminder, the three core functions of governors and the governing body are:

- **Accountability** – justification for the decisions that are being taken.
- **Oversight** – scrutiny and investigation of key decision making and performance.
- **Assurance** – confidence that the school is operating effectively and compliantly on a day-to-day basis and is on a stable footing.

Governor

Now, if you have been drawn to this question, I suspect you need to go back to the very start of this book. 😊

Let's start with a slightly more formal explanation – governors are responsible for overseeing the management side of a school: strategy, policy, budgeting, and staffing. They enable their school to run as effectively as possible, working alongside senior leaders and supporting teachers to provide excellent education to children.

Being a school governor is a commitment to attend governing body meetings that consider issues such as setting the school vision, mitigating financial risk, and scrutinising educational outcomes. They are also involved in the school community, acting as critical friends to the headteacher and senior leaders. Governors bring a wide range of skills and expertise from their professional lives to the governing board and schools benefit greatly from working with skilled volunteers.

I need to add a bit of a caveat here. The above is a good and broad description, but the specific responsibilities you have as a governor are shaped by your school – is it LA controlled or an academy, for example? I cover the role of a governor in much more detail at the beginning of this book, and I always recommend if you are new to the role in your school and didn't feel your induction made your responsibilities clear, then check out the school's 'scheme of delegation', which will identify which aspects of oversight and challenge are your responsibility.

GRT – Gypsy Roma Traveller

HLTA – higher level teaching assistant

Higher level teaching assistants can lead lessons when needed and work more closely with pupils on their learning requirements.

HMCI – Her Majesty's Chief Inspector of Schools

In essence, the HMCI is the head of Ofsted.

HNF - high needs funding

Also referred to as 'top up', high needs funding (HNF) is additional funding provided to support inclusion and meet the needs of children and young people with significant needs within mainstream schools and settings.

HoD - head of department

HofD - head of department

HofF - head of faculty

HofH - head of house

HoS - head of school

Head of school is a title often used instead of headteacher for schools within a multi-academy trust.

HPA - high prior attainers

High prior attainers (HPA) are students who show strong potential to achieve high-level outcomes across a range of subjects.

HPQ - Higher Project Qualification

A Higher Project Qualification is like an Extended Project Qualification (see EPQ) but is a Level 2 qualification available for younger pupils in Years 9 and 10 to do as preparation for their GCSEs and as a stepping stone to the EPQ. As with the EPQ, students doing an HPQ are expected to develop research skills, keep a production log, give a presentation on their research, and evaluate the process.

An HPQ is graded A* to C and is expected to take around 60 hours. Some schools use the HPQ as part of their programme to push more able students beyond their mainstream subjects.

HTPM - headteacher's performance management

It's probably easiest to just say HTPM is the head's appraisal process each year. There should be an appraisal panel of governors involved in the process as well as the appointment of an external advisor to assist.

Hybrid classroom

A hybrid classroom is a combination of physical face-to-face and online teaching and learning.

ICO – Information Commissioner's Office

The ICO is the UK's independent authority set up to uphold information rights in the public interest, promoting openness by public bodies and data privacy for individuals.

ICT – information and communications technology

IDACI

Bear with me on this one as it's quite complicated. The Income Deprivation Affecting Children Index (IDACI) measures the proportion of all children aged 0 to 15 living in income-deprived families. Although this only gets updated every five years it's important for schools because the IDACI data across your school's catchment has a direct impact on some of the funding your school receives. If we want to get a bit more technical, those calculations across your catchment are from local areas defined as 'lower layer super output areas' (LSOA) that each include approximately 1500 residents.

IDACI is a subset of a broader 'Index of Multiple Deprivation' (IMD) which measures deprivation across seven key areas:

- Income deprivation
- Employment deprivation
- Education, skills, and training deprivation
- Health deprivation and disability
- Crime
- Barriers to housing and services
- Living environment deprivation

The deprivation factor of the national funding formula (NFF) is based on this IDACI data alongside free school meals (FSM) eligibility data. This is the bit where your school will receive additional funding depending on how many of your pupils live in the most deprived IDACI areas.

IDSR - inspection data summary report

The IDSR is a web-based page showing key data for Ofsted inspectors to use during and in preparation for an inspection. The IDSR is designed to align with the school inspection handbook, so that areas of interest can be used to identify inspection trails.

IEB - interim executive board

This is hopefully not something you will encounter in your governance journey, but you will most likely encounter this where a school is struggling, and a decision is taken to replace the governing body. Where the school is under LA control, for example, they might appoint an interim executive board made up of experienced governors within the area to come in and support improvements at the school on a temporary basis.

IGCSE - International General Certificate of Secondary Education

An IGCSE is equivalent to the GCSE qualification that is taken by students in Years 10-11 in the UK.

The IGCSE is the international version of this academic qualification as it's available in many countries around the world. In the UK, the IGCSE is typically taught at international schools or private schools, rather than at state schools.

INSET - in-service training

All teachers have access to INSET in schools, helping them to refine their teaching and management skills. In essence it is time set aside for training and development that is provided within working hours.

ISR - individual school range

The individual school range (ISR) is the range of seven consecutive spine points on the head's salary scales, within which the head of a school can be paid. It is calculated by several factors, such as size of school, challenge of roll, etc. There are no longer statutory pay spine points within a range, but they are useful as a checkpoint when calculating leadership remuneration.

ISTE

One for our US readers, but also growing in popularity for European educators, ISTE stands for International Society for Technology in Education. Often the first reference is to their annual conference held in June each year, which moves around the US, but beyond that event they offer a membership with a wealth of professional development (see PD) opportunities with certification.

As ISTE (2022) explain it themselves, 'ISTE Certification for Educators is the only vendor-neutral, internationally recognized credential for educators who have demonstrated mastery of the [Educators section of the ISTE Standards]. ISTE Certification focuses on pedagogy, not on tools or devices, and is designed to change your educational practice, whether you're a classroom educator, instructional designer, library media specialist, technology coach or in another role. The programme combines 14 weeks of professional learning with a six-month portfolio application and review process, and recipients can apply to receive up to four graduate-level credits for their participation.'

You can find out more at www.ISTE.org

ITT - initial teacher training

Initial teacher training (ITT) is one of the most common pathways to gain qualified teacher status (see QTS).

IWF - Internet Watch Foundation

The Internet Watch Foundation (IWF) monitor the publication of content online linked to child sexual exploitation. If the incident/report involves sexual images or videos that have been made and circulated online, the victim can be supported to get the images removed by them.

KPI - key performance indicators

A performance indicator or key performance indicator is a type of performance measurement. KPIs evaluate the success of an organisation or of a particular activity in which the organisation engages.

KS1 - key stage 1

Key stage 1 covers Years 1 and 2 in an infant or primary school for ages 5 to 7.

KS2 - key stage 2

Key stage 2 covers Years 3 to 6 in a primary school for ages 7 to 11.

KS3 - key stage 3

Key stage 3 covers Years 7 to 9 in a secondary school for ages 11 to 14.

KS4 - key stage 4

Key stage 4 covers Years 10 and 11 in a secondary school for ages 14 to 16.

KS5 - key stage 5

Key stage 5 covers Years 12 and 13 in a secondary school for ages 16 to 18.

LAC - looked-after child

A looked-after child (LAC) is a child who has been in the care of their local authority for more than 24 hours. They are also often referred to as children in care. Each UK home country has a slightly different definition of a looked-after child and follows its own legislation, policy, and guidance. But in general, looked-after children are:

- living with foster parents
- living in a residential children's home or
- living in residential settings like schools or secure units.

Scotland's definition also includes children under a supervision requirement order. This means that many of the looked-after children in Scotland are still living at home, but with regular contact from social services.

There are any number of reasons why children and young people enter care, including:

- The child's parents might have agreed to it - for example, if they are too unwell to look after their child or if their child has a disability and needs respite care.
- The child could be an unaccompanied asylum seeker, with no responsible adult to care for them.
- Children's services may have intervened because they felt the child was at significant risk of harm. If this is the case the child is usually the subject of a court-made legal order.

A child stops being looked-after once they are adopted, return home, or turn 18. As an aside, local authorities are still required to support children leaving care at 18 until they are at least 21.

LADO - local authority designated officer

The local authority designated officer (LADO) is the person who should be notified when it's been alleged that someone who works with children has behaved in a way that has harmed or might harm a child, or has possibly committed a criminal offence against a child.

Lagged funding

Lagged funding is a term used to describe funding based on the previous year's schools census data. For example, funding for 2022 to 2023 for most academies was based on census data from the autumn 2021 census.

LGBTTQQIAP - lesbian, gay, bisexual, transgender, transexual, queer, questioning, intersex, asexual, and pansexual

LGPS - Local Government Pension Scheme

Link governor

A link governor is a governor who is assigned to 'link' with a particular faculty or take responsibility for a specific subject that they can investigate and research with relevant staff and then feed back to the local governing body. You might have link governors for key subjects, safeguarding, wellbeing, and so on.

LLE - local leader of education

LLE refers to headteachers designated by a local authority, in line with National College standards, as able to provide school improvement support to other heads and schools. (Since 2017, see SLE.)

LMS - learning management system

A learning management system is the system used to track student progress, results, and their broader activity while at school. Typically, this is one single system used across the school, trust, or district. Often their functionality overlaps with, or is entirely replaced by, an MIS system (see MIS).

Local Offer

The Local Offer was introduced by the Children and Families Act 2014. Every local authority must prepare a Local Offer and it should detail all the provision that is available in the local area, and neighbouring areas. The Local Offer should be particularly targeted at services that can be accessible to children and young people with special educational needs but should also contain useful information for all families. Guidance requires that the Local Offer is more than simply a directory of services, and should contain information such as eligibility requirements, waiting lists and availability.

LOTE - languages other than English

LSA - learning support assistant

A learning support assistant (LSA) helps children and young people who need support within the classroom. They assist the teacher to help children with extra learning needs so they can make the most of their education. The role is very similar to that of a TA, but typically LSAs are assigned to an individual child with needs, whereas a TA works more with the teacher to manage the class as a whole or with small groups. I should add there is no fixed rule; plenty of TAs provide 1:1 support for learners too.

LSCB - local safeguarding children board

Local safeguarding children boards (LSCBs) were established to place the responsibility for safeguarding and promoting the welfare of children on a statutory basis. In 2019 they were replaced by local Safeguarding Partners.

MA&T - more able and talented

The term 'more able and talented' is used to refer to pupils who are more able across the curriculum and those who show particular ability or aptitude in one or more specific areas.

Makaton

Makaton is a language programme that uses signs, speech and symbols to enable people to communicate. It supports the development of essential communication skills such as attention, listening, comprehension, memory and expressive speech and language.

Makerspaces

Often linked to delivery of STEAM, makerspaces encourage students to try, fail, and try again. Makerspaces are a hands-on method for STEAM learning, giving students space to explore science, technology, engineering, arts, and mathematics through practical projects and activities.

Managed move

A 'managed move' is defined as a formal agreement between two schools, a child, and their parents/carers. It allows a child at risk of permanent exclusion to have a trial transfer to another school on a dual registration basis, or to permanently move directly to their new school.

MASH - Multi-Agency Safeguarding Hub

The Multi-Agency Safeguarding Hub (MASH) works to keep children safe. It is a county-wide partnership that supports children and young people in need. It brings key professionals together to facilitate early, better-quality information sharing, analysis, and decision making, to safeguard vulnerable children and young people more effectively.

MDS - midday supervisor

The midday supervisors are responsible for securing the safety, welfare and behaviour of students during the lunchtime break. They tend to manage behaviour in the canteen and out on the playground while staff are having their lunch.

Members

Top of the multi-academy trust structure, alongside planning the strategic direction of your trust, members help to ensure that academy trustees are exercising effective governance by utilising a range of powers including being responsible for appointing and removing academy trustees. Think of the three levels of governance in your MAT as being members, trustees and governors.

Metacognition

It sounds complicated but in essence it's thinking about thinking, being reflective and reflecting on your learning experience.

MFA - Master Funding Agreement

'The Master funding agreement is the contract between the Secretary of State for Education under section 2, of the 2010 Academies Act and the Multi Academy Trust. The funding agreement specifies how the academy trust and schools within the academy trust should be run' (Smart Multi Academy Trust, n. d.).

MFL - modern foreign languages

This is the umbrella term for your department teaching French, German, Spanish and other languages in the school.

MIS - management information system

An MIS is designed so that all school staff - from data administrators and teachers to students and parents - have a central place to capture, report and assess data easily through a clear, intuitive interface.

MLD - moderate learning difficulty

'Children described as having moderate learning difficulties experience great difficulty in acquiring basic literacy and numeracy skills, despite receiving suitable help. They have general developmental delay, which means that they reach developmental milestones much more slowly than their peers do, and learn much more slowly. They are likely to have reached below level 2 of the national curriculum at the start of senior school. They may also have speech and language delay, difficulty in concentrating and underdeveloped social and emotional skills' (The Good Schools Guide, n. d.).

MPS - main pay scale

For classroom teachers - MPS points are from M1 to M6.

MSI - multi-sensory impairment

'Multi-Sensory Impairment (MSI) means that a child or young person has impairments with both sight and hearing. Their sensory loss may be present at birth or acquired later. Most children and young people with MSI will have some useful vision and hearing; however there are some who are completely deaf and blind. There are a number of terms used to describe MSI including deafblind, dual-sensory impaired and dual sensory loss' (Kirklees Council, 2022).

NAHT - National Association of Head Teachers

NAPTA - National Association of Professional Teaching Assistants

NASBM - National Association of School Business Management

NASEN - National Association for Special Educational Needs

NASUWT - National Association of Schoolmasters Union of Women Teachers

NB - non-binary

Non-binary is an umbrella term for gender identities that are not solely male or female - identities that are outside the gender binary.

ND - neurodivergent

The formal definition of neurodivergent is differing in mental or neurological function from what is considered typical or normal (frequently used with reference to autism spectrum disorders); not neurotypical.

NEET - not in education, employment or training

NEET is the classification for young people aged between 16 and 24 who are unemployed and not receiving education or vocational training. There is a particular focus on children aged between 16 and 18 and schools do report on NEETs from their cohort on departure at the end of Year 11 or 13.

NFF - national funding formula

The government uses the national funding formula (NFF) to work out your school's 'notional' core funding allocation. However, it's worth noting your actual allocation is based on a local funding formula from your local authority (LA), who bring all the funding into a pool and take a percentage to offset their costs of support and (where agreed locally) retain some funds to support other related services in the region.

NGA - National Governance Association

Hopefully you have already come across the National Governance Association (NGA). If you haven't, they are a great resource for all things school governance (after this book of course 😊).

You can find out more at: www.nga.org.uk

NLE – national leaders of education

The formal DfE description is that NLEs are outstanding headteachers who, together with the staff in their national support school, use their skills and experience to support schools in challenging circumstances. After a review by the NLE advisory group in 2020 recommending a smaller group of high-quality NLEs, a revised and more focused cohort of NLEs will be appointed for 2022-23, made up of headteachers who have experience of turning around schools and who can provide school improvement capacity.

NLG – national leaders of governance

National leaders of governance deliver external reviews of governance and support for schools and academy trusts through the National Leaders of Governance programme, funded by the Department for Education (DfE) and managed by the National Governance Association (NGA). Boards can also self-fund NLG support.

Designated NLGs are experienced governors, trustees, governance professionals, advisers and consultants from across England. Each NLG has demonstrated the substantial governance experience and expertise needed to carry out the role to a high standard through a rigorous and externally moderated assessment process.

Nolan Principles

The Nolan principles set out the ethical standards anyone should adhere to when working in the public sector.

They are referred to as 'The Seven Principles of Public Life' and were first issued by the Committee on Standards in Public life (CSPL) back in 1995. As you might have guessed, they are named after the then chair of the committee, Lord Nolan. These same principles apply to anyone undertaking a role in education, including as a governor, trustee, or member.

There are seven principles:

- **Selflessness**: Holders of public office should act solely in terms of the public interest.
- **Integrity**: Holders of public office must avoid placing themselves under any obligation to people or organisations that might try inappropriately to influence them in their work. They should not act or take decisions in

order to gain financial or other material benefits for themselves, their family, or their friends. They must declare and resolve any interests and relationships.

- **Objectivity**: Holders of public office must act and take decisions impartially, fairly and on merit, using the best evidence and without discrimination or bias.
- **Accountability**: Holders of public office are accountable to the public for their decisions and actions and must submit themselves to the scrutiny necessary to ensure this.
- **Openness**: Holders of public office should act and take decisions in an open and transparent manner. Information should not be withheld from the public unless there are clear and lawful reasons for so doing.
- **Honesty**: Holders of public office should be truthful.
- **Leadership**: Holders of public office should exhibit these principles in their own behaviour and treat others with respect. They should actively promote and robustly support the principles and challenge poor behaviour wherever it occurs.

You should always be mindful of these in your role as a school governor and remember, should you find yourself as part of a disciplinary process for any member of staff at your school, upholding these values will be part of your considerations.

NOR - number on roll

The number of students currently enrolled at your school, sometimes used as a subset to reflect number on roll in a class or similar.

NPQ - National Professional Qualification

Different National Professional Qualifications (NPQs) are available for teachers and leaders who want to develop their knowledge and skills in specialist areas of teaching practice. There are four leadership NPQs in senior leadership, headship, executive leadership and Early Years leadership, and four NPQs for teachers and leaders who want to develop their expertise in specialist areas of teaching practice.

The leadership NPQs are:

- NPQSL: Senior leadership - develop your leadership knowledge and expertise to improve outcomes for teachers and pupils in your school.
- NPQH: Headship - develop the knowledge that underpins expert school leadership and apply it to become an outstanding headteacher.
- NPQEL: Executive leadership - develop the expertise you need to become an outstanding executive leader, leading change and improvement across your group of schools or multi-academy trust.
- NPQEYL: Early Years leadership - develop expertise in leading high-quality Early Years education and care, as well as effective staff and organisational management.

The four NPQs in specialist areas of teaching have been designed with both classroom teachers and leaders in mind. They are:

- NPQLTD: Leading teacher development - learn how to become a teacher educator and successfully support teachers in your school to expand their skills.
- NPQLT: Leading teaching - learn how to lead the teaching and learning of a subject, year group or phase.
- NPQLBC: Leading behaviour and culture - learn how to create a culture of good behaviour and high expectations in which staff and pupils can thrive.
- NPQLL: Leading literacy - learn how to effectively teach and promote literacy across the whole school, year group, key stage or phase (DfE, 2022d).

NQT – newly qualified teacher

Newly qualified teacher (NQT) was the status of a teacher in their first full year of teaching. This status was replaced in 2021 with the new early career teacher (ECT).

NTP – National Tutoring Programme

In response to the disruption caused by the pandemic, the National Tutoring Programme offers highly tailored tuition support for your students. It is intended to help those whose education has been most impacted by Covid. This is currently available (as of August 2022) but may well cease in the coming months.

NUT - National Union of Teachers

Ofsted - Office for Standards in Education

If you are a governor in a school, I guarantee you will have heard of Ofsted. If you are about to embark on a new role as a governor, then the most simplistic summary is that Ofsted are the people that come and check you are operating your schools to an expected standard, undertaken by way of an inspection.

A summary can be found at gov.uk: 'Ofsted is the Office for Standards in Education, Children's Services and Skills. We inspect services providing education and skills for learners of all ages. We also inspect and regulate services that care for children and young people' (Ofsted, n. d.).

OJEU - Official Journal of the European Union

OJEU was used for placing and managing the procurement of high value tenders by schools, now replaced by the UK government's 'Find a Tender' process.

OT - occupational therapist

An occupational therapist provides support for physical and psychiatric conditions that limit a person's independence and daily living skills. OTs can be important in assessing and supporting children and young people with special educational needs.

PAN - published admissions number

In simple terms, the published admissions number is the number of children in each year group that your school's admission authority has agreed it can take. It's simply the agreed maximum capacity of your school. Typically this is based on a view of the number of students that can be safely taught in your school based on its size and facilities.

Where there are expansions to a school's infrastructure, new builds, etc., a school can apply to have their PAN changed. The LA needs to be notified or the PAN applied for through the Regional Schools Directorate for Academies and will require a formal consultation period with all stakeholders.

The PAN is also important to know as it comes into play when your school is full and there are appeals by parents for their child to join the school through your admission authority. I'd love to say when a school is full it's full, but appeals panels are a very variable experience and within the context of those appeal hearings the school will want to show its PAN and implication of going beyond that.

PD – professional development

Professional development (PD) is a is a mainstay in all schools. Sometimes it is offered by colleagues sharing best practices, sometimes by other leaders in your trust, or from outside speakers or vendors. It's such a broad term; having time to read relevant books, watch YouTube videos on top tips or best practice, or listen to relevant podcasts can all count as part of professional development.

PECS – picture exchange communication system

Picture exchange communication system is a communication system that uses picture tiles. PECS is primarily used for children and young people with autism, but it is a very effective tool for learners with communication or language difficulties. The use of PECs is a special educational provision.

Pecuniary interest

Much in the same way that a declaration of interest is raised at the start of a meeting where the topic being discussed might conflict with your personal or business interests, at the start of the academic year all governors, trustees and members should compete a pecuniary interests form, which simply lists your business interests and associations. This provides transparency and ensures you are not invited to attend discussions on anything that may cause you a conflict of interest.

PEP - personal education plan

A personal education plan is used for looked-after children (see LAC). It is prepared by the local authority, and it tracks the educational support provided for the young person and what progress they are making. The PEP is used for all looked-after children, not just those with special educational needs. If the looked-after child has special educational needs, the PEP should state this, set out what those needs are and what special educational provision is needed.

If a child or young person has a Statement of special educational needs or an education, health and care plan (EHCP), their PEP can be included within it.

PermEx - permanent exclusion

Permanent exclusion of a student from the school is what many of us years ago would refer to as being expelled. It is the decision of the head to permanently exclude a child, but there is always a right of appeal. If this is made, then a panel of three governors will typically sit to hear the appeal and either uphold or reverse the head's decision. See your appeal policy for details.

PFA - Preparing for Adulthood

Young people with SEND should have equal chances as they move into adulthood. Preparing them for life as an adult and establishing their goals is essential to ensuring they have a good quality of life. Preparing for Adulthood (PFA) identifies four pathways that young people should pursue: employment, independent living, social and community inclusion, and health and wellbeing. These should be addressed in the young person's education, health and care plan from the age of 13, with long term goals identified that can be worked towards.

PFI - private finance initiative

Private finance initiatives (PFI) were a programme to attract private sector funding into major school estate projects. I'm probably speaking out of turn, but in most cases this has simply left schools with long-term repayment schedules.

PGCE – Postgraduate Certificate in Education

The Postgraduate Certificate in Education (PGCE) is a one- or two-year higher education course in England, Wales and Northern Ireland that provides training to allow graduates to become teachers within maintained schools.

PISA – Programme for International Student Assessment

Tests are given to 15-year-old students in a number of OECD (Organisation for Economic Co-operation and Development) countries on mathematics, science, reading, financial literacy, and collaborative problem solving. First done in 2000 and repeated every three years, the PISA tests are used to provide an international league table of highest performing education systems.

See www.OECD.org/pisa/

PiXL – Partners in Excellence Club

I'm a big fan. PiXL is a partnership of thousands of schools, colleges and alternative education providers spanning KS1-5. Their aims are to improve life chances and outcomes, influence school leaders and to help equip them to be agents of change. As well as providing collaborative data gained from across their membership, they also provide classroom strategies, ideas and resources designed to have a positive impact on achievement, character, and culture.

Find out more at: www.pixl.org.uk

PLASC – pupil-level annual school census

PLASC is a digital collection of pupil and school level data provided by all maintained sector primary, middle, secondary, nursery and special schools in January each year.

PLN – personal learning network

Although some define it as a 'professional learning network', PLN typically refers to your work colleagues or education connections made on social media or through organisations. During the pandemic the role of platforms like Twitter and Instagram were and continue to be heavily used by educators to share ideas and seek advice from peers.

PMLD – profound and multiple learning difficulty

'A diagnosis of a profound and multiple learning disability (PMLD) is used when a child has more than one disability, with the most significant being a learning disability.

'Many children diagnosed with PMLD will also have a sensory or physical disability, complex health needs, or mental health difficulties' (NHS, 2015).

PNA – pupil number adjustment

Where an academy is initially funded based on estimated pupil numbers, they are included in the ESFA's annual PNA exercise during the academic year. The pupil number adjustment exercise determines whether adjustments are required to bring initial funding allocations (estimates) into line with the actual pupil numbers that schools record in the autumn (October) school census.

PPA – preparation, planning and assessment time

PPA is an allocation of time each week during which a teacher has cover to be away from the classroom to undertake other essential activities.

Prevent duty

In essence, the Prevent duty aims to safeguard people from becoming terrorists or supporting terrorism. As a governor it is your role to monitor your school's compliance with the Prevent duty. You could do this as a full governing body or have a link governor with specific responsibility. You would need to:

- Oversee relevant policies to make sure they reflect the requirements set out in Prevent.
- Ensure staff have appropriate training in Prevent.
- Ensure all governors have also read the Prevent guidance.
- Make sure the school has good protocols in place to address any issues with families and promote positive British values.
- Check that any visiting speakers are appropriately selected, supervised, and challenged if necessary.
- Make sure the school considers policies and procedures from your local safeguarding partners.

Privacy – data

Data privacy, sometimes also referred to as information privacy, is an area of data protection that concerns the proper handling of sensitive data including – most importantly – personal data (students and staff) but also other confidential data, such as certain financial data to meet regulatory requirements (think GDPR) as well as protecting the confidentiality data.

In our schools, that can cover everything from where our students' personal information is stored, who has access to it and how secure it is, making sure we don't use apps that might use that personal data for other purposes, through to processes in place to ensure we don't send information about one student to the wrong parents, and much more.

Progress 8

Progress 8 is a type of 'value-added' measure that indicates how much students at a secondary school have improved over a five-year period when compared to a government-calculated expected level of improvement. In other words, how well have they done based on what we statistically expected them to achieve.

It takes a pupil's performance in relation to their peers at primary school level, compares it with their performance at GCSEs (see Attainment 8 score) and then, after some fancy calculations, establishes whether the student has progressed at, above or below the expected level.

The scores for individual children are not published but they are grouped together to get an average for your school's overall P8 score.

A score of zero means that, on average, students in your school performed as well at GCSEs as other students across the country who achieved similar results originally at the end of key stage 2.

A score above zero means that, on average, students at your school made more academic progress than those students across the country who achieved similar results at the end of key stage 2.

A score below zero means that, on average, students at your school made less progress than students across the country who achieved similar results at the end of key stage 2.

Just to be clear, if your school has a negative Progress 8 score, it doesn't mean there was no progress, but rather that your students made less progress than their peers across the country. Also, this score is dependent on an accurate starting score at the end of Year 6 and does not include the full breadth of subjects across the curriculum.

PRU – pupil referral unit

See AP. An alternative provision school/PRU provides education for children of compulsory school age who are unable to attend a mainstream or special school, sometimes because they are disengaged from education, at risk of/have been permanently excluded and where additional nurture and support is needed.

PSCHE – personal, social, citizenship and health education

PSHE – personal, social, health and economic education

Personal, social, health and economic (PSHE) education is a school curriculum subject in England that focuses on strengthening the knowledge, skills, and connections to keep children and young people healthy and safe, and to prepare them for life and work. Some PSHE topics include relationships and sex, health and wellbeing, drugs and alcohol, financial education, the importance of physical education and diet, and other topics.

PSP – pastoral support plan

A pastoral support plan (PSP) is used in schools to help develop social, emotional, and behavioural skills. A PSP should identify targets for the child to work towards. The child and their parents should be involved with the preparation of the PSP.

PTA – Parent Teacher Association

Parent Teacher Associations (PTA) are an active part of school life for schools across the country. Many thousands of parents volunteer to join in with PTA activities at their child's school, giving their time and energy to fundraising and working in partnership with the school.

Pupil premium (PP)

We can start with the easy definition: pupil premium (PP) is funding to improve education outcomes for disadvantaged pupils in schools in England.

In terms of eligibility, it is paid to schools for students who are eligible for free school meals or have been eligible in the past six years (see Ever 6 FSM) or at a higher rate for students who have been adopted from care or have left care. It is paid to the local authority for any children who are in care with them.

The important bit for governors is (and actually there are a few bits so bear with me), firstly, the funds are paid to the school. They are not personal budgets so don't have to be spent student by student, but it is expected that it will be used specifically for support and interventions for your pupil premium qualifying cohort. The three key areas that are recommended for focus are:

- High-quality teaching, such as staff professional development.
- Targeted academic support, such as tutoring.
- Wider strategies to address non-academic barriers to success in schools, such as attendance, behaviour, and social and emotional support.

But that is by no means exhaustive, and schools will use PP funds to cover the costs of trips for some students, clothing, and all sorts of other initiatives to ensure they are supported. As a governor, however, you want to be satisfied there are bespoke interventions being funded by your PP and that existing staff costs and resources are not just being assigned to the pupil premium pot.

I did say there was more than one bit! In return for these funds, schools must show how they're using their pupil premium funding by publishing a statement on their website about how it is used (in detail) and the impact it has on the attainment of disadvantaged pupils. They will also be measured through inspections by Ofsted and through published performance tables. I would encourage you as a governor to go to your school website, find the school's pupil premium report, check it is up to date and ensure that it identifies where the funds have been spent, how impact was measured and what evidence the school has to support this. It's also a handy check to ensure your school website is up to date and that your pupil premium report, amongst others, is easy to find. I always used the 'night before' Ofsted inspector checking out your school website seeing out of date statements and reports still live. It doesn't set a good impression.

If you do have the pleasure of an Ofsted visit, then as a governor they will likely ask you what your pupil premium funding is for this year and how you know it is being well spent. You have been warned.

Check out this link for more information: www.gov.uk/government/publications/ pupil-premium/pupil-premium

QTS - qualified teacher status

The professional status you need to obtain to teach in state-maintained schools in England and Wales. QTS is normally awarded after successful completion of an initial teacher training course.

Quorate

A 'quorum' is the minimum number of governors/trustees that must be present at a full governing board or committee meeting in order for official decisions to be made. When a quorum is present, the meeting is said to be 'quorate'. Normally it requires at least half of the committee members to be present, but depending on your constitution it could be two thirds.

R&R - recruitment and retention

As the name almost hints, recruitment and retention (R&R) is a payment made to help recruit and subsequently retain a valuable addition to your staff. It's outlined in the School Teachers' Pay and Conditions document (STPCD) and in essence, if you are struggling either due to supply or competition to secure an amazing physicist or linguist, you have some flexibility to try to incentivise them to come and join your school, either with a one-off upfront recruitment payment or an ongoing retention allowance. I suspect in the coming years this will be an increasingly frequent part of job offers given the diminishing pool of experienced teachers to recruit from.

RI - requires improvement

This is linked to an Ofsted judgement after an inspection of your school. I'd love to hope you never have to discuss this term but it happens, and as always, it's how you address it moving forwards that really matters.

RAISEonline

A tool provided to support reporting and analysis of student data for supporting improvement. RAISEonline closed on 31 July 2017. The new Analyse School Performance (ASP) replaced it.

Reserves

These are the available carried forward (unspent) funds an academy or trust has from previous years. Under the Academy Trust Handbook, trustees are reminded that they must approve a balanced budget, taking into account brought forward reserves. Academy trusts are expected to maintain reserves, as they are standalone charitable companies.

The handbook also states that the board of trustees must notify the ESFA within 14 days if proposing a deficit revenue budget for the current financial year which it cannot address after considering unspent funds (reserves) from previous years.

Ring-fenced

A term you will likely hear during school finance meetings and relating to certain funding you receive. In essence, ring-fenced funds are not funds you can choose to spend as you wish but are specifically linked to being spent for a particular purpose. Those restrictions define your ring fence. Your funding for something like pupil premium or PE and sport premium has a defined ring fence as to where they can be deployed. Similarly in recent years, 'catch-up' funding could only be used for explicit activities and if it was not used, it had to be returned.

Risk register

As we know, risk is inherent in everything a school or academy trust does. It is a requirement within the Academy Trust Handbook that academy trusts manage risks to ensure their effective operation, and they must maintain a risk register.

A common approach is to consider risks under the following categories:

- **Internal risks** - these are the risks over which the academy trust has some control, by managing them through internal controls/additional mitigating actions. Some handy examples of these kind of risks include health and safety risks and data security.

- **External risks** - these focus on big external events (I can think of one big one over the last few years) and then consider how to make the trust more resilient to them. Recent examples include the response to the pandemic and dealing with extreme weather.

- **Strategic risks** - these are the risks to the delivery of the trust's core objectives. For example, common ones right now include loss of key staff, inability to recruit, academic outcomes, risk to reputation and so on.

- **Project risks** - these are the risks associated with any critical projects the trust may be involved in. For example, delays on the delivery timescale for a new building, not gaining sufficient student numbers to make a new school or expansion viable, etc.

Once any kind of risk has been identified, it is important to quantify it so you can compare all risks identified consistently. Measurement typically consists of assessment, evaluation, and ranking. The aim of assessment is to better understand each instance of risk and how it could affect the trust. At a high level you should consider two key measures to score a risk:

- the **likelihood** (or probability) of it occurring, and
- the **impact** (or severity) if it did occur.

Give each of those measures a score of one to six (six being the highest risk) and multiply them together to get a risk score. You can then sort all your risks and see which have the biggest potential for impact. I could write lots more on this, but it would likely get a bit complicated, so the important thing to remember is that your risk index (your spreadsheet with all the risks identified) should be reviewed and updated regularly and it should be brought to, and discussed at, your trust board on a regular basis.

RJ - restorative justice

A tricky one to explain. Restorative justice (RJ) can be defined by its core objective: namely that when one student has harmed another, the most useful response is to try to repair the harm done.

Restorative justice in schools can involve holding conferences between the perpetrator and the victim with a mediator, peer mediation and of course informal restorative approaches by staff. In essence it focuses more on mediation and acknowledgement of wrongdoing rather than punishment.

RPA - risk protection agreement

In a school context, a risk protection agreement (RPA) is an alternative to purchasing commercial insurance, which may save time and money. There is a fixed cost per student for RPA cover for academies. At the time of writing it is £21 per student with a similar cost for LA-maintained schools. RPA covers everything from your various employer, professional and governor liability, business interruption (think disaster recovery plan), cyber disruption, accidents and of course any damage claims.

RSC - Regional Schools Commissioner

The Regional Schools Commissioner's office was renamed in Sept 2022 to the Regional Schools Directorate.

RSE - relationships and sex education

SACRE - Standing Advisory Council on Religious Education

The role of SACRE is to support and give advice to the local authority, schools, teachers and parents/carers on matters that are related to collective worship and religious education in community schools.

Safeguarding Partners

The Safeguarding Partners in relation to a local authority area in England are made up of (a) the local authority, (b) a clinical commissioning group, and (c) the chief officer of police within the local authority area.

The three safeguarding partners should agree on ways to coordinate their safeguarding services; act as a strategic leadership group in supporting and engaging others; and implement local and national learning including from serious child safeguarding incidents.

Safer recruitment

First up, this is something I encourage all governors to undertake and renew every two years. In most schools I would expect to see this as a requirement for any governors who are taking part in a staff recruitment process.

In summary, safer recruitment training for governors is training to help you safely recruit the right staff and volunteers for your school ensuring they are safe to work with children and young people. Safer recruitment courses for governors only take a few hours and within them you will cover:

- Developing safer recruitment policies and procedures for your organisation.
- Preparing to recruit.
- Selecting the right people to interview.
- Carrying out thorough background checks.
- Responding to concerns identified through background checks and assessing risk.
- Responding to inappropriate behaviour and allegations of abuse.

To find out more visit: www.gov.uk/government/publications/safeguarding-children-and-safer-recruitment-in-education

SALT - speech and language therapists

Speech and language therapists (SALT) help with the development of speech, language, and communication skills. A speech and language therapist can be important in the development of the physical processes of speaking or swallowing, as well as the acquisition and development of language and communication skills.

SAMS – statutory assessment and monitoring service

The SAMS team will be based at your local authority and are responsible for coordinating the statutory process in relation to education, health and care (EHC) needs assessments and the review of EHC plans.

SATs – Standard Assessment Tests

If you are a primary governor, you will likely have come across these as your main checkpoints in a child's academic performance. The Standard Assessment Tests (SATS) are used to evaluate each child's educational progress at the end of Years 2 and 6. They make comparisons between your children versus the average attainment expectations for their respective age group nationally.

Key stage 1 SATs take place at the end of the infants stage in Year 2. The assessments are carried out internally by the teacher and they evaluate ability in reading, SPaG (spelling, punctuation and grammar) and maths.

Key stage 2 SATs are a more formal process than key stage 1 and take place near the end of Year 6. The tests also cover reading, SPaG and maths. The papers are marked externally not internally like the KS1 SATs.

Scaffolding

Scaffolding is breaking up the learning into chunks and providing a tool or structure with each chunk, in essence adding extra layers of support into a lesson or topic.

Scheme of delegation

If you are a governor in a multi-academy trust you need to know what this is, and you definitely need to have a copy. I would argue it's one of the most important things to understand as a governor or trustee.

I have shared more details earlier in the book, but as a basic summary for the benefit of this section, a scheme of delegation sets out where responsibilities and accountabilities sit within your multi-academy trust's (MAT's) structure. For example, it will indicate whether a task is the responsibility of the board of trustees, local governing bodies (LGBs), headteachers or other SLT.

SCITT - school centred initial teacher training

This is normally a partnership of schools and sometimes other organisations that deliver teacher training places in your area. There is quite a bit of turmoil in this area at the moment with the DfE changing who is able to deliver teacher training, so it's worth checking if your school engages with a SCITT for finding new staff.

SDP - school development plan

This probably sounds more formal than it needs to, but your school development plan (SDP) is a strategic plan for improvement. It should bring together, in a clear and simple way, the school priorities, the main measures it will take to raise standards, the resources dedicated to these, and the key outcomes and targets it intends to achieve.

SEAL - social and emotional aspects of learning

The term social and emotional aspects of learning (SEAL) refers to five broad areas. These include self-awareness, managing feelings, motivation, empathy, and social skills. If a child or young person requires support with their social and emotional aspects of learning, they may have special educational needs requiring special educational provision.

SEF - self-evaluation form

An SEF is an online form that helps schools evaluate their own performance and is used by Ofsted inspectors prior to an inspection to help identify where they might need to focus their efforts.

The school self-evaluation form (SEF) is the school's evaluation of how it is performing in key areas, including: effectiveness of leadership and management; quality of teaching, learning and assessment; personal development, behaviour, and welfare; and outcomes for children and other learners. It also includes key data on the context of the school and its cohort with a breakdown of its ethnicity profile, children with additional needs and so on. Ask to see a copy of yours.

SEL - social and emotional learning

Using the definition from CASEL (Collaborative for Academic, Social and Emotional Learning) SEL is defined as the process through which children and adults acquire and effectively apply the knowledge, attitudes, and skills necessary to understand and manage emotions, set and achieve positive goals, feel and show empathy for others, establish and maintain positive relationships, and make responsible decisions (CASEL, 2022).

SEMH – social, emotional and mental health

Social, emotional and mental health (SEMH) is a broad term used to define a range of different needs children may have at any given time. This term has gained more and more attention as teachers and parents have become aware of the increased awareness of mental health in children and the impact that this can have on their wellbeing and ability to learn.

SENDIASS

A nice catchy one, SENDIASS stands for the 'Special Educational Needs and Disabilities Information Advice and Support Service'.

SFVS – Schools Financial Value Standard

The Schools Financial Value Standard (SFVS) is a requirement for all maintained schools, who must submit it to their local authority (LA) every year.

It helps to provide your governing board (and the LA) with reassurance that your school meets the standards necessary to achieve a good level of financial health and resource management. Your chair of governors will need to review and sign your SFVS before submission to the LA.

SIG – school improvement group

Sometimes SIG is also used to refer to a 'special interest group'.

SIMS – Schools Information and Management System

SIMS is a central IT system that records all data associated with each child in your school, including attendance, behaviour, academic progress, any areas of concern and individually relevant information. It is the most widely deployed school information and management system used in the UK, although in recent years it has changed ownership a couple of times and has been losing market share.

Single central record

The single central record (SCR) is a statutory requirement under KCSIE for all schools and academies. They must keep and maintain a single central record of recruitment and vetting checks for all staff (including relevant volunteers, supply teachers, agency and third-party staff, and teacher trainees on salaried routes). It will also contain similar information for the governing body of your school.

SIP - school improvement partner

You may well come across an SIP as part of your headteacher or trust leadership performance management. They work with school leaders to support, challenge and validate self-evaluation. They are able to support teaching and learning reviews and are often used to support the development of leadership at all levels.

Skills matrix

A skills matrix is a framework used to map governors' skills. It's a grid that contains information about skills and their evaluation. It is used to manage, plan, and monitor existing and desired skills for recruitment.

SLASC - School-level Annual School Census

SLASC is an annual, statutory census that takes place every January from independent schools. It captures a range of key information including:

- their contact details
- the number of pupils on the attendance register
- the number of teaching staff
- the courses of study
- the number of pupils with special educational needs (SEN)
- the number of pupils in local authority care
- annual fees
- details of accommodation
- the number of staff members who have joined or left since the last census
- the school's proprietors.

SLE - specialist leader in education

Specialist leaders in education (SLEs) are typically outstanding middle and senior leaders in positions below the headteacher, with at least two years' leadership experience. They have a particular area of expertise (such as a subject area, Early Years, behaviour, etc.) and a successful track record of school improvement. Officially the DfE no longer designates SLEs.

SLT - senior leadership team

The SLT would normally consist of the headteacher, any assistant and/or deputy heads, the school business manager and any other appropriate and experienced members of teaching staff. It would be key members of the SLT that you would expect to see regularly at local governing body/academy committee meetings.

SLT - speech and language therapy

Not to be confused with the acronym for your school's senior leadership team, SLT is also used within the context of providing speech and language therapy for children requiring additional support.

SMSC - spiritual, moral, social and cultural

SNSA - Scottish National Standardised Assessments

Since 2017, children in Scotland have completed Scottish National Standardised Assessments (SNSAs) in literacy and numeracy in years P1, P4, P7 and S3.

SOFA - statement of financial activities

The statement of financial activities is part of the academy's accounts return (AR) undertaken each year.

SPaG - spelling, punctuation and grammar

And you thought with SPaG I was going to make a bad joke about bolognese!

Sport premium

To use its full name, the PE and sport premium is funding for primary schools to support the government's 'school sport and activity action plan' to ensure children have access to at least 60 minutes of sport and physical activities each day. Schools must use the funding to make additional and sustainable improvements to the quality of the PE, physical activity, and sport they provide. They are also required to make a summary of funding and how it was spent available on the school website, so make sure you take a look.

SQA - Scottish Qualifications Authority

The SQA is the non-governmental body responsible for accreditation and awarding in Scotland.

STEAM

STEAM is the abbreviation for science, technology, engineering, arts and maths. It is sometimes referred to as STEM when the arts element is excluded.

STPCD - School Teachers' Pay and Conditions Document

The School Teachers' Pay and Conditions Document (STPCD) is an annually published document that forms a part of the contract of all teachers and headteachers in maintained schools in England and Wales. The document is binding in all maintained schools and local education authorities.

Summative assessment

This is where evaluating a student's learning is done at the end of their topic or unit. An exam or essay would be good examples. See formative assessment for the alternative.

Synchronous learning

A term that has become much more common since the arrival of the pandemic. Within the context of remote learning, synchronous learning is real-time teaching and learning where instructors and learners participate in instant two-way communication.

TA – teaching assistant

Teaching assistants (TAs) play a vital role in supporting teachers in the classroom. They can cover everything from getting the classroom ready for lessons, listening to children read, reading to them, helping children who need extra support to complete tasks, helping teachers to plan learning activities and completing observations and assessments. More experienced TAs can also qualify as higher level teaching assistants (HLTA).

Terms of reference

Terms of reference are written guidelines that clarify the role, purpose and responsibilities given to a committee. These will exist for all your committees including the main boards.

The Key for School Governors

The Key for School Governors is definitely one of your go-to resources for all things school governance, other than this book of course! It's a fantastic resource that your school can join and provides advice, guidance, templates, and anything governance-related for your school. It also includes resources for school leaders, for safeguarding and broader CPD.

Find out more at www.thekeysupport.com

T Levels

'T Levels are new 2-year courses which are taken after GCSEs and are broadly equivalent in size to 3 A Levels. Launched in September 2020, these courses have been developed in collaboration with employers and education providers so that the content meets the needs of industry and prepares students for entry into skilled employment, an apprenticeship or related technical study through further or higher education.

'T Levels offer students practical and knowledge-based learning at a school or college and on-the-job experience through an industry placement of at least 315 hours – approximately 45 days.

'The courses are available at selected colleges, schools and other providers across England' (DfE, 2022b)

At the time of writing, one of the key barriers to speedy adoption by providers has been the challenge in them finding enough employer partners who can offer the 300+ placement hours per student that are required.

TLR – teaching and learning responsibility

A TLR is an area of extra responsibility assigned to an individual teacher and attracting additional salary. The salary scales for TLRs are published in the same way that pay scales are in the School Teachers' Pay and Conditions Document (see STPCD).

The STPCD provides for three broad bands for the values of TLR payments: TLR1, TLR2 and TLR3. There can be more than one level of TLR payment within each TLR band. Each school will decide for itself the number of levels of TLR payments within the two bands and the specific values of the TLR payments at each level.

Typically, a school might have three levels of a TLR1 - denoted as TLR1a, TLR1b and TLR1c, with the TLR1c reflecting the highest value. A lower level (and value) TLR 2a and TLR2b would also be available.

To qualify for a teaching and learning responsibility payment of any kind, teachers' duties must include a significant responsibility that is not required of all classroom teachers and that:

- is focused on teaching and learning
- requires the exercise of a teacher's professional skills and judgement
- requires the teacher to lead, manage and develop a subject or curriculum area or to lead and manage pupil development across the curriculum
- has an impact on the educational progress of pupils other than the teacher's assigned classes or groups of pupils; and
- involves leading, developing and enhancing the teaching practice of other staff.

The STPCD statutory guidance makes clear that responsibility for other teachers or accountability for a subject area should be linked to TLR1 or TLR2 payments or leadership group posts.

TOIL – time off in lieu

Time off in lieu, otherwise known as TOIL, is when an employer offers time off to workers who have gone above and beyond their contracted hours. Essentially, it serves as an alternative to pay, meaning that any overtime hours worked by an employee can be taken as part of their annual leave.

Top slice

The term top slice is normally used within a multi-academy trust (MAT) to reference the percentage of each individual school's revenue that is taken to offset the costs of running the central operations of a MAT. As a rule, a typical top slice figure is between 3% and 5% and naturally means the larger schools in your trust would be contributing more to the overall pot, but equally likely taking more time to support.

In some cases, MATs can be much more prescriptive and adapt that top slice percentage to reflect the status of the school. So perhaps a school that has RI (requires improvement) status needs greater support and interventions, and therefore has a higher top slice percentage for a period.

While common in most MATs, some trusts do not use the top slice model and simply choose to recharge on a service level for all resources and support used. It is worth noting that too large a top slice (without clear justification) will likely raise challenge and scrutiny from the Regional Schools Directorate or any trust inspection.

Transitions

Normally transitions in schools are when a child moves from one phase of their education to the next, most commonly moving from Year 6 (primary) to Year 7 (secondary). The more effectively schools can support the process, the quicker a child is settled and progressing in their new school.

Trust board

The trust board is the accountable body ultimately responsible for the education of children and young people across all of your schools. The trust board, made up of your appointed trustees, also determines the responsibilities it delegates to your academy committees/local governing bodies. See your scheme of delegation for more information.

TUPE – Transfer of Undertakings (Protection of Employment)

The Transfer of Undertakings (Protection of Employment) Regulations 2006 (TUPE Regulations) apply to most situations in which staff working in schools are transferred between employers. The TUPE Regulations safeguard employees' rights when the business or organisation in which they are employed changes hands.

Typical examples include:

- The transfer of staff from the employment of the school to a contractor, e.g. cleaning, catering, extended services staff.
- The transfer of staff into the school, e.g. staff of local pre-school when an agreement is reached to bring this provision into the school; or the school decides to cease to use a contractor and to bring its catering or cleaning provision in-house.
- The transfer of staff from one contractor to another contractor when a school decides to let a contract to a different service provider.
- The transfer of all employees when a school converts to become an academy.

UCAS – Universities and Colleges Admissions Service

UDL – Universal Design for Learning

Universal Design for Learning (UDL) recognises that if students can't access information, they can't learn effectively. It is a teaching approach that works to accommodate the needs and abilities of all learners and eliminates unnecessary hurdles in the learning process. So, in a UDL classroom, materials are accessible for all types of learners. Students have many options for reading, including print, digital, text-to-speech and audiobooks.

UIFSM – universal infant free school meals

Universal infant free school meals (UIFSM) provides funding for all government funded schools to offer free school meals to pupils in reception, Year 1 and Year 2.

Unconscious bias

How a person thinks can depend on their life experiences and means they have beliefs and views about other people that might not be right or reasonable. This is known as 'unconscious bias' and includes when a person thinks better of someone because they believe they're alike, or thinks less of someone because that person is different to them. For example, they might be of a different race, religion, or age.

UPR – upper pay range

The upper pay range is for classroom teachers – the scale is structured from U1 to U3.

The STPCD explains that qualified teachers can apply to the UPR. To qualify, teachers must meet criteria set out in the school's pay policy based on criteria from the Department for Education (DfE).

UPS – upper pay scale

The upper pay scale is also known as the upper pay range.

URG – under-represented groups

URN – Unique Reference Number

The Unique Reference Number (URN) is assigned to every school by the national education department (state and independent schools).

UTC – university technical colleges

UTCs are academies for 14-19-year-olds. They provide technical education that meets the needs of modern employers. They offer technical courses and work-related learning, combined with academic studies.

VG – voluntary grammar school

A grammar school in Northern Ireland.

Virement

A virement is the process of moving funds between budget headings, something that often happens in your school budget when there is perhaps an underspend in one area and a request for something outside of budget elsewhere.

Virtual school

As the name implies, it is more of an approach rather than a physical entity. Virtual schools work with all their looked-after children (LAC) in their region, as if they were within a single school, liaising with the actual schools they attend, tracking the progress they make and supporting them where needed. Virtual schools report on the performance of their children as a cohort to ensure they are not further disadvantaged.

My Secret #EdTech Diary

John Catt Educational Publishing - ISBN 978 1 913622 63 3 - July 6 2021 - 260 pages.

With 30+ years' experience developing and using EdTech products, distilled down into an easy-to-read format, *My Secret #EdTech Diary* aims to get you thinking about the past, present and future role of educational technology and how it influences and shapes our education system. *My Secret #EdTech Diary* reflects on the history of EdTech, lessons learned pre- and post-Covid, best practice suggestions, how to select the right solutions, and the questions you need to consider before pursuing your digital ambitions.

With unique insights from an educator's and vendor's perspective, advice for budding EduPreneurs, guidance for schools considering how to co-produce technology solutions with vendors and how to make the right choices, AI aims to shine a light on educational technology through the widest possible lens. With links to research, insights from trusted peers, quick ready-reckoner checklists, questions you need to be asking, and voices aligned from the sector, this book aims to get you up to speed and thinking big-picture EdTech.

In an effort to make EdTech accessible for all, the book is written to give even those considering themselves a technology novice an easy and accessible overview of EdTech, unpicking what some of the trending terms mean, what questions to ask and to help them join the debate, confident and engaging from a position of knowledge.

★★★★★ 'A revelation even for a seasoned EdTech creator.'

★★★★★ 'Jam-packed with useful and interesting content.'

★★★★★ 'An excellent, informative and accessible book.'

★★★★★ 'Raising the profile of digital in schools - the right tool for the job!'

★★★★★ 'Absolutely fantastic. This book is a secret that I will be sharing.'

★★★★★ 'An EdTech masterpiece.'

Thank you

I could and should add quite a big 'thank you' here, firstly for buying my book and making it all the way to the end. I really hope you found it interesting and it has given you a few more ideas, confirmations and questions for you to use in your role as an effective school governor.

I always like to thank **John Catt Educational** publishers (www.johncattbookshop. com) for supporting me in my endeavours and for publishing my books. Please check them out as they have an amazing array of books covering every educational topic you can think of. I'd also like to make special thanks to Natasha Gladwell who edited my book and did such a great job. Never underestimate the importance of a fab editor supporting you.

Most of all, I just want to thank everyone who has made the leap and voluntarily gives up their time to support our amazing schools and educators. We rightly should be proud of the value that our collective governance provides to our education system.

If (fingers firmly crossed) you found the book helpful, please leave a nice review on Amazon for me. If you didn't find it helpful, then hopefully you will be kind enough not to be too critical; I've done my best. Please also feel free to tweet a photo of you with my book. As you'll have seen from the previous page, I had so many lovely photos from my previous book launch, and I would love to emulate that. You can find me on Twitter as **@AlKingsley_edu** or on LinkedIn as plain old Al Kingsley. I'd love to connect and share ideas for future writing.

Thank you again, and I wish you every success on your governance journey.

Al.

References

CASEL. (2022) *What is social and emotional learning?* Available at: https://drc.casel.org/what-is-sel/

Committee on Standards in Public Life. (1995) *The Seven Principles of Public Life.* Available at: www.gov.uk/government/publications/the-7-principles-of-public-life/the-7-principles-of-public-life–2

Croner-i. (2015) *What does a partnership do?* Available at: https://app.croneri.co.uk/feature-articles/working-together-improve-behaviour-and-attendance

DfE. (2015) *The Prevent duty.* Available at: www.gov.uk/government/publications/prevent-duty-guidance/revised-prevent-duty-guidance-for-england-and-wales

DfE. (2017) *A Competency Framework for Governors.* Available at: assets.publishing.service.gov.uk/government/uploads/system/uploads/attachment_data/file/583733/Competency_framework_for_governance_.pdf

DfE. (2018) *Assessment without levels: qualitative research.* Available at: https://assets.publishing.service.gov.uk/government/uploads/system/uploads/attachment_data/file/918928/NFER_AWL_report.pdf

DfE. (2020) *Governance Handbook.* Available at: www.gov.uk/government/publications/governance-handbook

DfE. (2021) *Fair Access Protocols.* Available at: https://assets.publishing.service.gov.uk/government/uploads/system/uploads/attachment_data/file/1012993/FAP_Guidance.pdf

DfE. (2022a) *Education Inspection Framework.* Available at: www.gov.uk/government/publications/education-inspection-framework.

DfE. (2022b) *Introduction of T Levels.* Available at: www.gov.uk/government/publications/introduction-of-t-levels/introduction-of-t-levels#t-levels-what-they-are

DfE. (2022c) *Keeping Children Safe in Education*. Available at: https://assets. publishing.service.gov.uk/government/uploads/system/uploads/attachment_ data/file/1101454/Keeping_children_safe_in_education_2022.pdf

DfE. (2022d) *National professional qualifications*. Available at: www.gov.uk/ government/publications/national-professional-qualifications-npqs-reforms/ national-professional-qualifications-npqs-reforms#npqs-available

ESFA. (2021) *Academy Trust Handbook*. Available at: www.gov.uk/guidance/academy-trust-handbook

ESFA. (2022) *Academy trust risk management*. Available at: www.gov.uk/government/ publications/academy-trust-financial-management-good-practice-guides/ academy-trust-risk-management

FFT. (n. d.) *About FFT*. Available at: https://fft.org.uk/about-fft/

Governors for Schools. (2018) *A quantitative assessment of the work of the governors for schools charity*. Available at: www.governorsforschools.org.uk/ app/uploads/2020/02/GfS-Impact-Report-short.pdf

Governors for Schools. (2021) *Questions for governors to introduce the topic of staff wellbeing and mental health*. Available at: https://governorsforschools.org.uk/ news/questions-for-governors-to-introduce-the-topic-of-staff-wellbeing-and-mental-health/

Inside Government. (2020) What is the role of the designated safeguarding lead? Available at: https://blog.insidegovernment.co.uk/schools/what-is-the-role-of-the-designated-safeguarding-lead-dsl

ISTE. (2022) *ISTE Certification*. Available at: www.iste.org/professional-development/ iste-certification

Kirklees Council. (2022) *Multi Sensory Impairment*. Available at: www. kirkleeslocaloffer.org.uk/information-and-advice/a-z-of-specific-conditions/ multi-sensory-impairment-msi

Knightsmith, P. (2019) *Promoting positive mental health*. Available at: www.nga.org. uk/Knowledge-Centre/Pupil-success-and-wellbeing/Pupil-wellbeing/Mental-health/Promoting-positive-mental-health.aspx

National College for Teaching & Leadership. (2014) *Leading governors: The role of the chair of governors in schools and academies.* Available at: https://assets. publishing.service.gov.uk/government/uploads/system/uploads/attachment_ data/file/323830/leading-governors-the-role-of-the-chair-of-governors-in-schools-and-academies.pdf

National Governance Association. (2019) *Articles of association.* Available at: www.nga.org.uk/Knowledge-Centre/Governance-structure-roles-and-responsibilities/Academy-trusts/Guidance-Changing-Articles-of-Association. aspx

National Governance Association. (2021a) *Academy trusts: the role of members.* Available at: www.nga.org.uk/getmedia/1c2b9a16-d818-4dd7-bf54-c1efd452b590/MAT-Members-Guidance-16pp-(May-2021)-WEB-AW.pdf

National Governance Association. (2021b) *Recognising your governance professional.* Available at: www.nga.org.uk/getmedia/28f85833-d59c-4e04-9122-fe712b48ba82/nga-recognising-your-governance-professional-20210622. pdf

National Governance Association. (2022) *NGA skills audit.* Available at: www.nga. org.uk/Knowledge-Centre/Good-governance/Effective-governance/Governing-Board-Self-Review-(1)/Skills-Audit-and-Skills-Matrix.aspx

NHS. (2015) *Profound and multiple learning disability (PMLD).* Quoted in: EHP. (2022) What is specialist teaching of profound and multiple learning difficulties (PMLD)? Available at: https://ehp.org.uk/our-services/specialist-teaching/ profound-and-multiple-learning-difficulties-pmld/

Ofsted. (n. d.) *What we do.* Available at: www.gov.uk/government/organisations/ ofsted

Parsons, L. (2020) *Writing a digital vision for your school.* Available at: https:// digilinlearning.com/2020/04/12/writing-digital-vision-for-your-school/

Persona Education. (n. d.) *Persona skillsets and life skills.* Available at: www.persona-life.com/developing-over-20-life-skills-across-six-skillsets/

Puffett, N. (2010) *Government clarifies ban on Every Child Matters.* Available at: www.cypnow.co.uk/other/article/government-clarifies-ban-on-every-child-matters

Ribble, M. (2021) *Essential elements of digital citizenship*. Available at: www.iste.org/explore/digital-citizenship/essential-elements-digital-citizenship

Rose, E. (2022) *How can schools establish a culture of safeguarding?* Available at: www.sec-ed.co.uk/knowledge-bank/top-10-safeguarding-priorities-for-schools-attendance-child-protection-abuse-ofsted-mental-health-education-governors-curriculum-pshe-radicalisation

Smart Multi Academy Trust. (n. d.) *Master & supplementary funding*. Available at: www.smartacademies.net/master-supplementary-funding/

Spielman, A. (2018) *HMCI commentary: curriculum and the new education inspection framework*. Available at: www.gov.uk/government/speeches/hmci-commentary-curriculum-and-the-new-education-inspection-framework

The Good Schools Guide. (n. d.) *ASD – autism spectrum disorder*. Available at: www.goodschoolsguide.co.uk/special-educational-needs/types-of-sen/asd-aspergers-syndrome-and-autism

The Good Schools Guide. (n. d.) *EPQ (Extended Project Qualification)*. Available at: www.goodschoolsguide.co.uk/curricula-and-exams/extended-project-qualification

The Good Schools Guide. (n. d.) *Moderate learning difficulties*. Available at: www.goodschoolsguide.co.uk/special-educational-needs/types-of-sen/learning-difficulties

Wilkinson, N. and Long, R. (2019) *School governance: House of Commons Briefing Paper no. 08072*. Available at: https://researchbriefings.files.parliament.uk/documents/CBP-8072/CBP-8072.pdf

Zak, D. (2021) *'Nothing ever ends': Sorting through Rumsfeld's knowns and unknowns*. Available at: www.washingtonpost.com/lifestyle/style/rumsfeld-dead-words-known-unknowns/2021/07/01/831175c2-d9df-11eb-bb9e-70fda8c37057_story.html

Index

Cool tools for school

And finally, I did start the book by sharing that I have spent the last 30 years developing cool solutions for schools with the brilliant team at NetSupport (www.netsupportsoftware.com). It might be that one of these has a fit with your school's digital ambitions or plans. Anyway, it can't hurt to share, and it is my book after all. ☺

Solution for IT management, monitoring and safeguarding

NetSupport DNA is an easy-to-use solution that provides schools and trusts with the tools to manage technology across all platforms in the classroom and across the school, while safeguarding students and assisting with GDPR compliancy. Network managers, safeguarding leads and teachers all benefit from dedicated toolkits allowing them to achieve best practice.

NetSupport DNA provides schools and trusts with the tools to manage technology in the classroom and across the school, while safeguarding students and supporting teachers. Easy to install and use, NetSupport DNA offers a wealth of network and IT management tools for network managers to track, monitor and manage IT assets and endpoints across a school or entire trust – all from one central point. Armed with a complete overview of school IT activity, technicians can work smarter, while maintaining a secure and reliable network. From staying ahead of any potential IT issues before they escalate to automating tasks, NetSupport DNA not only helps save time but also boosts security and productivity. It also gathers a wealth of device and usage data to inform decision making and allow accurate planning of future IT spending and refresh plans. Helping schools to achieve best practice, NetSupport DNA also includes a safeguarding toolkit to help meet e-safety requirements, as well as optional classroom management tools to support a technology-enhanced teaching environment.

Safeguarding, filtering and e-safety

Maintain a safe learning environment for staff and students while meeting the latest government requirements with NetSupport DNA's dedicated safeguarding toolkit.

As technology increases in schools, it's essential they have the tools in place to protect students as they access online resources for learning, as well as being able to identify and support those with safeguarding issues. Designed to be operated independently of the IT team, NetSupport DNA's safeguarding toolkit provides both proactive and reactive tools. Developed with teachers, safeguarding leads, local authorities and the Internet Watch Foundation, the tools are relevant, effective and, most importantly, up to date – further enhancing schools' safeguarding policies. Being able to see what students are typing, searching for or copying across a range of safeguarding topics (e.g. cyberbullying, eating disorders, mental health, etc.) means staff can be aware of issues and have the right support in place, and status markers on triggered events show them the current stage of review. With language packs available to ensure safeguarding can be extended to an even wider group of students, NetSupport DNA's safeguarding module gives schools a welcome helping hand to keep students safe online.

Feature-rich classroom instruction and monitoring

With over 33 years' development expertise, **NetSupport School** is the market-leading and most feature-rich classroom instruction and monitoring solution available for multiple platforms across LAN and WAN.

With dedicated assessment, monitoring, collaboration and control features, all easily reached through its intuitive interface, NetSupport School allows teachers to leverage the full value of technology-enhanced teaching. Developed with teachers, for teachers, it has a host of easy-to-use tools available in just one click, plus three graded user modes (easy, intermediate and advanced) to support teachers' EdTech confidence and ensure there are as few barriers to its use as possible. As well as monitoring students' activity to keep them focused and safe, NetSupport School helps teachers to deliver a range of learning content formats and encourage interaction with tools such as online surveys, a student feedback mode, chat, message and a gamified Q&A module. Tools such as chat, help requests, sending out/collecting work in one click (and more!) help with social distancing in class – plus, its monitoring and collaboration tools even help teachers instruct students spaced over separate rooms. Developed with Ofsted best practice in mind, it's no wonder NetSupport School is the complete classroom management solution of choice.

Or if you want to head to the cloud...

Cloud-based classroom management, safeguarding and IT management... all in one solution

Super easy to set up and use, **classroom.cloud** is a cloud-based classroom management, safeguarding and IT management platform, providing the essential tools for engaging and protecting students as they learn in school or remotely.

classroom.cloud is all about simple, essential teaching tools to monitor and instruct in classrooms and with remote learners – as well as maintain student engagement and ensure they're on target for success! Teachers can easily connect to their students via pre-populated class lists and share their screen and audio to help explain lesson activities. During the lesson, they can use the thumbnail view to see the screens of all the students in the class and monitor activity. Setting 'allowed' and 'restricted' websites/applications lists, muting/unmuting audio on the students' devices and controlling USB and webcam use helps to keep everyone safe and on task. Teachers can also remotely control students' screens, interact with surveys and help requests, and give everyone a voice with chat and messaging tools. With no swapping between solutions for in-school and/or remote learning, it's a simple and effective way to provide continuity for students and teachers. The best bit for the IT team is that it's low cost and scalable to even the largest of MATs – as well as being super easy to set up, manage and maintain. There are hardware and software inventories to help technicians maximise their school's technology.

Keeping your students safe online – the safeguarding toolkit helps keep your online environment protected by monitoring concerning activity, identifying students at risk and spotting trends across multiple languages.

Keeping all your students safe as they learn online can be a challenge, but things just got easier with classroom.cloud's safeguarding toolkit! Schools can identify, support and help protect students at all times – no matter where they are. These powerful tools are perfect for helping inform your online safety strategy and school policies, as well as supporting the latest requirements.

Keyword and phrase monitoring: powered by over 14,000 phrases in multiple languages, schools can monitor the safeguarding words that students are typing (even in Microsoft Teams).

When a keyword or phrase is triggered, it populates a word cloud. This is a nice easy way to spot trending topics. The context of a triggered event is analysed (the device used, time of day, websites visited, applications used, history of alerts) and a risk index number is generated, helping staff to determine its severity. Schools can also link triggered events to their MYCONCERN and CPOMS accounts. Students can also report their concerns by sending a message in confidence to a trusted member of staff.

Students have instant access to a range of online support resources, covering topics such as FGM, drug addiction, grooming and bullying. Staff can also manage the pre-populated list and add any additional ones they feel are appropriate.

With its easy-to-use access permissions and reports that can be applied or changed as needed, schools can ensure only authorised staff have access to the most sensitive information. Images or screenshots can also be blurred to ensure maximum confidentiality.

EYFS and primary pupil journalling and assessment app

Low-cost, secure and easy to use, **ReallySchool** (award-winning app and online portal) helps teachers and TAs to capture and assess EYFS and primary pupils' learning and development quickly and effectively – while boosting parental engagement and supporting the continuation of learning at home.

Proven to save valuable time every day, ReallySchool offers a flexible and streamlined approach to capturing and assessing observations from EYFS and primary pupils. Teachers, TAs and practitioners can capture photos, videos and audio clips to provide key evidence of learning as it happens and assess against a range of different frameworks (which can be changed on the fly), subjects, learning areas and age bands in one observation – as well as selecting and changing the number of students taking part. Student learning journals and a wealth of reports display the progress of students, classes and year groups, helping school leaders to monitor whole-school teaching and learning. To help support children learning at home, teachers can send out home-learning activities and guidance directly to the parents' version of the ReallySchool app. Parents can also share achievements from home by sending videos, audio and photos. Teachers can use badges to acknowledge pupils' achievements, which can also be shared with parents to celebrate their success. Developed in close consultation with primary school teachers and TAs, ReallySchool offers real benefits for everyday use – and delivers more time for teaching!

Alerting and notification for lockdown and emergencies

Schools are fast realising the benefits of using mass notification solutions such as **NetSupport Notify** to boost school communication and support their emergency and lockdown procedures.

Using NetSupport Notify, schools can communicate effectively with staff and students using one-way alerts and notifications – sending them to desktop users across the school, those working remotely on school devices, and even to large information panels in halls and foyers. Alerts automatically take screen focus, meaning they can't be hidden, ignored or saved for later. The notifications can even be targeted to select groups and scheduled for maximum impact. Scaling to the largest of schools with multiple sites, NetSupport Notify also provides real-time status of notifications and acknowledgements [] as well as delivering pre-scheduled alerts. Simple to implement and use, and with fast and reliable alerts, NetSupport Notify helps ensure staff and students instantly have the information they need to work effectively and stay safe in any emergency situation.

Helpdesk and ticketing

Delivering effective and timely responses to IT issues is key to maintaining a reliable school IT environment. With **NetSupport ServiceDesk**, school IT support teams get the tools they need to do just that.

Easily integrated into a school's existing IT infrastructure, NetSupport ServiceDesk delivers the processes needed to help effortlessly track, organise, manage and answer the toughest support challenges. Providing effective support for users of IT assets is a priority for today's schools with their ever-increasing IT portfolios, and

NetSupport ServiceDesk's fully customisable and intuitive browser-based interface makes it easy for technicians to maintain both desktop and mobile platforms, while delivering robust workflow processes. As well as helping school IT support teams handle users' daily IT issues, NetSupport ServiceDesk will also highlight recurring IT problems - enabling them to identify and fix the root cause and ensure a productive working environment for everyone. Added to this, it supplies a wealth of management reports as well as providing a customer-friendly, self-service portal: all the tools needed to help technicians deliver support effectively.

Powerful multi-platform remote control and access

For schools wishing to take their remote support requirements to the next level, **NetSupport Manager** provides seamless and secure multi-platform access to workstations and servers across a school or trust.

NetSupport Manager has consistently led the way with innovative features to aid remote PC management. Designed to operate over your LAN, WAN or the internet, securely and without the need for firewall configuration, NetSupport Manager provides a single, high-speed solution for the remote management of critical systems, servers and users - with no need for third-party services or ongoing subscription costs. Adding to traditional one-to-one remote-control capabilities, NetSupport Manager excels as a one-to-many solution: from monitoring multiple systems in real time and showing the operator screen to multiple recipients for training, to file distributions across the network. Its enviable reputation for security sets it apart from others, with its use of activity logs, 256-bit encryption, smart card support, AD integration and more. It also enables IT teams to provide remote support to staff off-site and allows staff working remotely to access their work PC and applications safely and securely from home. What makes NetSupport Manager unique is its range of supporting tools to ensure maximum efficiency and, most importantly, its ability to minimise system downtime and lost productivity as support issues are being addressed - making it the perfect tool of choice for any IT team.

Just head over to www.netsupportsoftware.com/education-solutions/ to find out more.